Clarity in Everyday Life:
A Handbook and Guide

The Balanced View Team

Second Edition 2011
Balanced View Media: Mill Valley, California USA 2011

Based on a work at
www.balancedview.com.
ISBN 978-0-9843694-5-4

Clarity in Everyday Life:
A Handbook and Guide

TABLE OF CONTENTS

Section One: The Basics of Clarity in Everyday Life

Section Two: The Gifts of Open Intelligence

Section Three: Open Intelligence Expressed in Our Day-to-Day Lives

Potential; Fearless in the Face of Fear; Completely Count-on-Able; Total Relief

Section Four: Open Intelligence in Relationships

Section Five: Open Intelligence Pervaded by Peace

NOTE TO THE SECOND EDITION

We have been very encouraged by feedback from readers who have enjoyed and benefitted from the first edition of *Clarity in Everyday Life: A Handbook and Guide*, and it is with great pleasure that we are now able to bring out a revised and updated edition of the book.

As part of the ongoing effort in Balanced View to find the best possible language that speaks skillfully to the most participants, a shift in the use of language came about in 2011 that found great resonance. Whereas previously the terms "clarity" and "points of view" had been used in the texts, the new terms "open intelligence" and "data" spontaneously came into use and were received with great enthusiasm, as these new terms seem to speak to readers in an even more direct way.

As a result, all of the Balanced View books are being updated to include this new and very powerful language. The content of this book is the same as the first edition, and all the same chapters and sub-chapters are here—albeit with some slight changes in some of the titles and section headings. The main change is that of using the term "open intelligence" instead of "clarity" or "awareness," and "data" instead of "points of view."

The change in language should make the message of the book even more powerful and clear.

EDITOR'S INTRODUCTION

So often we face challenging circumstances in our lives and we are not sure what to do or where to turn. Our usual strategies of coping with the situations we face often have not worked before and continue not to work, and as a result we feel confused and irresolute. We struggle to find the best solution, but once a solution is envisioned and acted on, frequently we have to deal with the doubt, uncertainty and misgivings that surround the decision. The comings and goings of our lives seem to involve the endless appearances of problems that crave solution and the creation of numerous approaches to deal with those problems

However, no matter how prominent this scenario may have been in our lives, there is another choice. That is the simple choice to rely on the open intelligence that is the essence of all experience and to continue to return to that open intelligence for short moments, many times, until open intelligence becomes continuous. As our assurance in open intelligence increases through the commitment to taking short moments, our confidence in open intelligence naturally also grows, and the experiences that seemed so challenging to us before are no longer so challenging.

This book is meant to be a companion on the journey of gaining more and more assurance of inherent open intelligence through short moments, repeated many times, until continuous. The focus of the book is very practical, and the instruction given here is sensible and useful. Whether the topic is family life, intimate relationships, love, children, money, illness, afflictive states or finding peace in oneself and in the world, the trainings in the book point out over and over again that the resolution of data is the natural outcome of relying on open intelligence for short moments, many times, until open intelligence is obvious.

Each chapter has a principle theme, and within each chapter are sub-sections that deal with specific topics that follow the main chapter theme. The sections can be read separately or in sequence, but any of them can be read individually without reference to the other sections. The readers of this book are invited to go through and seek out relevant sections that are helpful and interesting for them personally.

It is very important to define the various words that are used in the text. The most important term is *open intelligence*, which is used very often throughout the book. Other terms that refer to the same essence pointed to by open intelligence include *clarity, awareness, the basic state, the fundamental nature of our being, natural perfection, total perfection, intelligent space, super-intelligence, super-completeness, self-perfected reality*, and *natural intelligence*.

The fundamental practice that is discussed throughout the book is that of *relying on open intelligence*. Whereas in previous books and texts the terms "resting as awareness" or "relying on clarity" were often used for this same practice, *relying on open intelligence* is a term that has shown itself to be much more direct and less subject to misunderstanding. Relying on open intelligence is the core principle of basing one's experience in open intelligence rather than in the data.

Over and over again, the phrase *short moments, many times* is used to convey the fact that one can rely on open intelligence in each and every moment, and one can continue returning to open intelligence for short moments over and over again until the practice becomes spontaneous.

The very important term *data* refers to all thoughts, emotions, sensations, experiences and any phenomena that appear in open intelligence. In previous Balanced View books the term "points of view" was used, but in the meantime many readers have come to find that "data" is a descriptive term that more accurately describes their experience. The key to understanding data is to see that they have no independent nature and are nothing other than the dynamic reflective energy of open intelligence. The two are inseparable like the color blue and the sky.

The material for this book comes from talks given by Candice O'Denver, the founder of Great Freedom and Balanced View. These talks were given in the US, Sweden and India and collected and transcribed by a dedicated team of volunteers. The material most relevant to everyday life issues was compiled, arranged and edited into its present form.

We, the editors, would like to most graciously thank Candice for this marvelous training and also the many other volunteers who made this book possible.

Section One
The Basics of Clarity in Everyday Life

THE INSTINCTIVE RECOGNITION OF OPEN INTELLIGENCE

CHAPTER ONE

SHORT MOMENTS OF OPEN INTELLIGENCE

What is a short moment of open intelligence? To know the answer to that question, stop thinking just for a moment. What remains? A sense of alertness remains. This is what open intelligence is: alertness that is open like a cloudless sky. One short moment of open intelligence is the instinctive recognition of unending open intelligence.

Thoughts, emotions, sensations and other experiences—data—appear within open intelligence just as a rainbow appears within space. In the same way that space and a rainbow are inseparable, thoughts, emotions, sensations and other experiences are inseparable from open intelligence.

When we stop thinking for a moment, we introduce ourselves to open intelligence, and before long we begin to notice that the open intelligence that is present when we are *not* thinking is also present when we *are* thinking.

All thoughts appear and vanish naturally like the flight path of a bird in the sky, and the peaceful open intelligence and alertness that is identified when we stop thinking is the basis of all those thoughts. It saturates all thoughts without exception in the same way that space is present in whatever appears within it. By relying on short moments of open intelligence, open intelligence becomes increasingly automatic. This may happen slowly or quickly.

Short moments of open intelligence can be likened to creating a string of pearls. Each pearl is added to the string with complete confidence that a complete string of pearls will be the result. It is the same with short moments. Just as stringing one pearl at a time leads to a complete necklace, by relying on always-present open intelligence for short moments again and again, those short moments become continuous in one's own experience. Once it becomes continuous, taking short moments is no longer necessary.

As open intelligence becomes more and more constant and unbroken, we find that it has an immense power that we never dreamt possible. There is the power to solve problems and the power to act skillfully in all situations. When it is recognized that this innate open intelligence resolves our personal problems, the conviction begins to emerge that it has the power to resolve the problems of the world as well. We are awed by how obvious open intelligence is and amazed that it has always been present within us, even though we may not have recognized it. It is of the greatest fortune to know it now.

THE BENEFITS OF SHORT MOMENTS

One very common idea is that open intelligence is separate from thoughts, emotions, sensations and other experiences. However, only from the vantage of incomplete knowledge is there an apparent separateness. From the vantage of open intelligence there is no separateness at all.

An excellent illustration of open intelligence existing within all data is that of butter existing in cream. When cream is churned the butter becomes obvious, even if it had not been obvious before. Just as churning cream cannot fail to produce butter, short moments of open intelligence bring to light the unending open intelligence that is evident in moment-to-moment perceptions.

At first it may seem like nothing is happening when the cream is churned, but with persistence the churned cream

3

ps a buttery texture and then butter itself appears. The cream is pervaded by butter, and this becomes evident through churning. Likewise, short moments of open intelligence, repeated again and again, spontaneously become continuous open intelligence in all situations, and irreversible open intelligence is seen to be present at all times.

In the beginning we remember a short moment of open intelligence, but maybe then we sometimes forget, and this is normal. However, we must never give up on these brief moments of open intelligence. As momentary as they may be in the beginning, they are having a tremendous impact. The benefits may not be so obvious initially, but we must continue to stay interested in open intelligence. We must have the kind of resolve that says, "I will never give up on short moments of open intelligence!"

By the power of short moments we begin to discover more and more a sense of clarity that fills us with soothing, powerful energy. By carrying on with short moments, whenever we remember to do so, the moments naturally begin to last longer. As the moments of open intelligence grow longer, we find that our mind and body are much more at ease. We begin to notice a soothing quality and increasing beneficial energy in our daily life. Never underestimate the power of this simple practice. It is the most powerful force on earth.

UNENDING OPEN INTELLIGENCE

Short moments of open intelligence are acknowledged as unending clarity. The initial short moments grow longer, and along the way it dawns on us that these moments are actually revealing permanent, unending open intelligence. We discover that open intelligence is available all the time. This dawning is similar to the way the sunrise illuminates the entire landscape.

Before the sun rises, the elements of the landscape are lost in the dark, but once it rises, everything is seen clearly.

This can be likened to being lost in the dark of thoughts, emotions, sensations and other experiences until we are introduced to open intelligence. When the sun of open intelligence rises, it increasingly provides a balanced view of all thoughts, emotions, sensations and other experiences. We find the balanced view of open intelligence *within* the data. The unending clarity in each moment provides complete mental and emotional stability, insight, natural ethics, empathy, skillfulness in all situations and the consistent power to fulfill creative intent for the benefit of all.

Short moments repeated again and again *do* become continuous. By putting this into practice, we attain deep confidence in the power of short moments to bring benefit to our lives. We keep it simple: short moments, many times. Unending open intelligence becomes increasingly obvious until it is evident at all times. As our clarity in all things develops, we see that we aren't as complicated as we may have thought. In fact, we're quite simple.

The power of open intelligence shows us that thoughts, emotions, sensations and experiences are simply data appearing within open intelligence. This can be illustrated by the way planets and stars appear within the expanse of space; similarly, data appear within open intelligence. Just as space is unaffected by any event within it, open intelligence is unaffected by data.

We empower ourselves with short moments, and we see that this very same potential for empowerment is within everyone. Based on our own experience we come to the conclusion that by everyone empowering themselves with short moments of open intelligence, the people of the world can unify themselves and be the force that brings about world peace.

When we hear about open intelligence we might ask, "Well, what is it?" Open intelligence is in fact the basis and origin of the question itself. The words appear in open intelligence, and the question and the questioner are both equally rooted in open intelligence. Yet, initially it's quite unlikely that we would be able to identify open intelligence, because we've never learned what it is in our own experience. There has to be an introduction to open intelligence and some sense of what it is before one can gain assurance in it. That introduction to open intelligence could happen spontaneously by being in the presence of someone who already has assurance of open intelligence. But it isn't the person who is doing something to us; it is just that we are sensing ourselves, maybe for the first time.

Another introduction to open intelligence can come about by simply stopping thinking just for a moment. Anyone can stop thinking for a moment, and when we stop thinking for a moment, all that's present is alertness, cognizance and a balanced view, and that's what open intelligence is. When we look at that alertness, we can't say that it is anything. It is an intelligence that sees every single datum that appears within it *as it*. Whether there's a thought or no thought, open intelligence is equally the space of both. Open intelligence isn't only present in no-thinking; it is also present in thinking.

We need to rely on some means of becoming familiar with and certain of open intelligence, and for most people the easiest way to do that is through short moments repeated many times, until short moments become continuous Whenever we remember to, we take a short moment of identifying that alertness, stability and balanced view that is at the basis of all data. We stop thinking just for a moment—a short moment of open intelligence—and we repeat that many times. To "repeat it many times" means that we return to it repeatedly, again and again, in an uncontrived, unforced way.

As we do this we become more familiar with the inseparable nature of open intelligence and data. Just as the color blue and the sky are inseparable or the sun's rays and the sun are inseparable, data and open intelligence are inseparable. Through short moments repeated many times, we become more certain in open intelligence, we really see that this alertness is present all the time and that we can return to it again and again.

In this simple, easy way we become confident in short moments, and in time the practice becomes spontaneous and continuous. It is in fact continuous from the beginning, but we just haven't recognized it. As we acknowledge open intelligence more and more, the acknowledgement becomes continuous. We begin to see that all data appear in, of, as and through open intelligence.

THE MOST IMPORTANT CHOICE

For many of us it is quite challenging to rely on open intelligence when there are disturbing data streams. It is important to see that even very disturbing states arise within ever-present open intelligence. It is important to acknowledge that the basis of all the data streams is open intelligence. We choose for open intelligence to be obvious to us or not. This moment-to-moment choice is the most important choice we make. *need more info on this!*

Practically, this is how it works: when disturbing data arise, we rely on a short moment of unending open intelligence. Over time, by the power of the short moment growing longer, there is instinctive open intelligence regardless of what type of data arise. Much to our surprise we find that all of these disturbing data streams rest in open intelligence.

By the power of short moments of open intelligence, all data flow on by. The here-and-now immediately clears itself without any effort or anything needing to be done. Just as the light of the

7

sun outshines all planets and stars during the day, the power of the innate clarity of open intelligence outshines thoughts, emotions, sensations and other experiences. In open intelligence there is profound intelligence, and we are introduced to it right on the spot, wherever we are. It's this simple: if we do not rely on open intelligence, we never find this clarity.

Open intelligence, relaxed and enormously potent, is the source of life satisfaction and flourishing, complete mental and emotional stability, profound insight into the nature of existence, increased intelligence, spontaneous altruism, morality and ethics, superb skillfulness and consistent power to benefit all

major claim

INSTINCTIVE RECOGNITION

Your own natural beneficial state and beneficial energy don't need to be cultivated or developed. If you try to cultivate or develop it, all you're doing is engaging in more streams of data of trying to make things a certain way. There's no way to create beneficial energy. It's already present, and in the simple acknowledgement of it, it becomes evident.

This simple acknowledgement doesn't occur on a verbal, mental or intellectual level. The recognition is instinctive, and this is the meaning of the term "instinctive recognition." It means that you instinctively realize your own native condition just *as it is.* When you relax with all the ideas that you have about everything—including your ideas about what awareness, clarity and open intelligence are—then your disposition is completely serene and open. There is no need to get all wrapped up in thinking about all our data streams; there is just the easygoing acknowledgement of everything *as it is.*

In that disposition, instinctive recognition becomes really easy. Relax body and mind completely—that's what instinctive recognition is. It doesn't mean just kicking back on the couch, although it can also mean that. It means that, throughout the full

range of experience, body and mind are completely relaxed and at ease as the basic state of natural perfection. It already is that way, so it does not need to be made that way. Even if you were running a twenty-six mile marathon, your body and mind would be completely relaxed. *talk more about this.
How do you stop avoiding, huh)

By relaxing your hold on the way you think everything has to be, you allow for everything equally. You begin to experience everything *as it is* and you experience yourself exactly as you are. There may be all kind of thoughts, emotions and sensations that you've been avoiding, but once that avoidance stops, you just are as you are—openhearted and open-minded. The unflinching pervasiveness of the here-and-now, nakedly seeing, is simply *as it is*. It allows for everything equally, with nothing to change.

Unless we really start to gain confidence in that instinctive realization, what has been said here will only be a bunch of words. We can't arrive at this confidence intellectually; it has to be arrived at instinctively. It is instinctive because it is beyond thought and reason. We can understand it intellectually, but that won't take us all the way. The words may be fantastic and they may evoke an expansive sense of clarity and open intelligence, but unless we take short moments of relying on the open intelligence that we have been introduced to, we won't have the astonishing benefits of pervasive open intelligence in our lives.

OPEN INTELLIGENCE AS THE BASIS

CHAPTER TWO

OPEN INTELLIGENCE AND DATA

It's important to be introduced to open intelligence—to the fundamental clarity and intelligence that exist within everyone. This is the fundamental intelligence of nature itself, including human nature. What is that fundamental intelligence? It is alert, clear and cognizant; it's our power to know everything. Whatever appears within open intelligence—all the descriptions of our life or our data sets—is inseparable from it. By relying on open intelligence rather than data, we have complete perceptual openness in all experience.

Most of us learn to focus on data and rearrange them in order to have a good life. We never learn about the clarity of open intelligence, which is the balanced view in which all data appear. We don't learn that there is something about us that is profound and which has mastery over all the data. We have been trained to think that by rearranging the data we'll be good people; however, most of us never achieve that to our satisfaction, and we always feel that we've fallen short.

No matter what our data are, once we are introduced to open intelligence, we can see that all the data appear within that view. This means that as we go along in everyday life we're drawing on a completely different type of intelligence than we had while we were totally focused on rearranging data. Our fundamental intelligence is alert, clear and cognizant, and it's easy to rely on the intelligence of a balanced view rather than on all the data.

First we are introduced to open intelligence, then we increasingly see that the data appear within open intelligence and are inseparable from open intelligence—like the sky and the color blue are inseparable. At first it might seem like the data are something other than open intelligence, but by relying on open intelligence, we see that it pervades all data. When a thought occurs, we can see that it appears in open intelligence, it endures in open intelligence, it disappears in open intelligence and its entire process is open intelligence.

For most of us the primary motivation is to arrange circumstances so that we can feel good. We want to provide for our food, clothing and shelter, and maybe we want to provide that for some other people as well, but it can be an all-consuming ordeal if we get involved with all the data surrounding those needs.

No matter what we're involved in, the basis of human life is the same for everyone and everything: open intelligence. By relying on open intelligence, it's easy to live; by relying on data, it isn't easy to live. It is a totally simple equation.

RELYING ON OPEN INTELLIGENCE

The research carried out in the field of quantum physics has shown that all phenomena are inseparable. This is the way nature is—inseparable—and it is impossible to pluck anything out of nature. Where would it go? The nature of the many worlds and what is beyond the many worlds is within open intelligence. Open intelligence contains all, and the data that appear are non-separate from open intelligence.

It's impossible to take any datum out of open intelligence. It's impossible to be outside open intelligence; open intelligence simply is. We rely on open intelligence moment-to-moment for short moments, repeated many times until open intelligence becomes obvious. This is very simple: relying on open intelligence—with data appearing, enduring and resolving in open intelligence—for short moments, many times until the short moments become continuous.

In a sense we've used short moments for many other things we do automatically, like brushing our teeth or tying our shoes. It may have been awkward when we were first learning about moving the toothbrush around in our mouths or trying to get the laces tied on our shoes. It seemed it would take us forever to learn the skills, but now because of our familiarity with those things, we do them completely without thinking. It is through the same sort of process that we grow familiar with open intelligence. Just as we learned our name by continually acknowledging that name, we learn about open intelligence by acknowledging open intelligence.

By relying on the totally spacious expansiveness of open intelligence, we're able to rely on our fundamental basic intelligence to solve problems. Whereas we had difficulty resolving problems before, increasingly we grow to see we can solve every problem that comes up from the spaciousness of open intelligence.

SIGNS OF ASSURANCE

Initially we might not recognize open intelligence all the time, but through continuing with short moments, open intelligence becomes more and more obvious. We begin to have more mental and emotional stability because we are letting the data flow on by; we don't need to jump into the story and get distracted by the data. We're a lot more relaxed and carefree about the data, and we're no longer seeing data as something to base our lives on. By the power of open intelligence we start to see that data are like empty sky. It comes to the point where we don't even notice the data anymore. They flow on by without distraction.

If we rely on our peaceful nature, swiftly and surely we will find something about ourselves that we never dreamt present. We begin to see signs of assurance in everyday life. What are

12

the signs of open intelligence assurance? They are the power to recognize our own instinctive open intelligence more and more, and with it to come to complete mental and emotional stability, insight, compassion and superb skillfulness and consistent power to fulfill creative intent of benefit to all.

These signs of self-arising open intelligence are present in everyone. In that sense we are all gifted children who have these profound gifts in us. All we need to do is access them, and the golden key is to be found in short moments of open intelligence, repeated many times until open intelligence becomes obvious.

We do not need to engage in all sorts of practices in order to get to these signs of assurance. All the signs of assurance are already present in a short moment, just like heat is already present in the sun. The reality of our own nature is our greatest strength, and it is very simple and unelaborated. Why turn it into a big project?

What we really want to focus on is these short moments of relying on open intelligence, and in a short moment of open intelligence all powers are already present. These are the powers we want to look to, because they guarantee our own well-being as well as the well-being of others. They guarantee unity and peace in us and in the world around us. Even if we think it is of value to get into special states of bliss for our own satisfaction, eventually we'll see that ultimately there is nothing to be gained in that. We want the *practical* signs of open intelligence assurance. Having those, we're no longer fooled by all these other data.

SIGNS OF MASTERY

When the mastery of our peaceful nature—our innate intelligence—is deeply abiding in us in all circumstances, we enter into a way of living that is very powerful and filled with tremendous energy. We are able to effortlessly do what most people can't even imagine doing. This is a sign of mastery: the ability to accomplish amazing feats that seemed undoable.

When I first had a clear idea of the way I wanted to direct my life—and that was all that I had—I didn't really know what it would look like to bring that vision about. All kinds of thoughts occurred such as, "Gee, I can't do this. How is this going to happen? I'm just one person." If I had stayed only with those thoughts, I would have never done anything. However, in the fire of commitment that was present, the all-accomplishing power to fulfill creative intent became available.

This is what it means to achieve mastery: we have the power to bring about incredible benefit, and each and every day we know exactly what actions need to be taken to bring that benefit about. Day by day everything that is needed is known, and the power to act on it is present.

The manifestation of these aspects of mastery in the lives of individuals can come about in many different ways. For example, it's possible that training people about open intelligence and their peaceful nature is not what you are interested in at all. Maybe instead you are a scientific researcher and you want to find a cure for a disease. By the power of the mastery of open intelligence, you'll be able to make enormous advances in finding a cure for that disease. Whether you're dealing with environmental issues, getting clean water or nourishing food to everyone on the planet or establishing peace on earth, the power to accomplish these things comes about through the mastery of our peaceful nature.

This same power to act skillfully is also present when people come together in an organization, and there are certain masterful qualities and activities that an organization can exhibit. The first one is the power to introduce people to their natural intelligence. The second is the power to bring about confidence and certainty in that intelligence to the point of mastery. A third demonstration is having written offerings that help guide people in discovering their innate open intelligence. Along with this is the ability of the organization to provide a 24/7 support system to anyone who wants that support.

At some point, in a very natural way the commitment to gain certainty in our innate open intelligence and peaceful nature bears fruit. We're no longer collapsed in an obsessive self-focus, and through the tremendous release of energy that comes about by the instinctive recognition of open intelligence, we naturally and spontaneously want to be of benefit to all. Great changes in the world can come about, because mastery of open intelligence allows access to a tremendous level of skill and intelligence that isn't otherwise known.

THE DEMONSTRATION OF OPEN INTELLIGENCE

From the very first short moment of open intelligence, we experience full blown clarity and compassion. Many of us have led most of our lives never hearing about what is authentic about ourselves, but when we do hear it we start to relax into our authentic nature without any effort on our part. We feel, "Ah ha, this feels right. There is something about this that is so soothing." From that very first moment of the soothing energy of open intelligence, there is the tremendous release into clarity and compassion.

In each short moment of open intelligence we harness the powers of clarity. Why haven't we had these powers of clarity before? Because we have been too wrapped up perpetuating all of our stories about the way things are and the way we are. Initially in the practice of short moments many times it's important to not be distracted by the stories; we return to short moments of open intelligence again and again, as often as is possible.

Clarity and compassion are what is authentic, and this is what we want to be able to exhibit in our lives. We want to see more and more of the balanced view of clarity and compassion in ourselves so that those powers can benefit others.

A wonderful metaphor for the powers of clarity and compassion is the sun and sunshine. Just like sunshine naturally emanates from the sun and can't be stopped in any way, so too clarity and compassion shine forth from open intelligence. We know whether or not we are gaining confidence in open intelligence by the presence of clarity and compassion—by becoming more stable mentally and emotionally, by having more insight into ourselves and into other people, and by experiencing the warmth of compassion. We can see in subtle and overt ways whether or not we are becoming more skillful in life.

There are a lot of fancy things that can be said about open intelligence, but what we want to see is the demonstration of its balanced view in our lives. This is true evidence of confidence in open intelligence.

MASTERY OVER PHENOMENA

The worst kind of addiction and the worst kind of cult is the one that we belong to without knowing it! We might say, "I'm not addicted to anything; I'd never join a cult," while in fact we may be participating in full blown addiction and complete cultish behavior by believing in the independent nature of data. Life based on data is a life of powerlessness, helplessness, unmanageability and addiction to the idea that appearances have an independent existence.

Once there's an understanding of the true nature of data—that data appear without truly existing independently and that they arise without ever being separate or apart from open intelligence—then there's an understanding that everything that appears is like a mirage. Just like we can't get anything from a mirage, there's nothing whatsoever to be gotten from appearances. No matter how desperately thirsty we are, we're never going to get a drink from a mirage.

It's the same with looking for well-being in data. All of these mirage-like data are like last night's dream; there isn't anything there. Whether you're waking, dreaming or sleeping, the idea of "you" and the entire cast of characters and parade of images you experience have never been any kind of solid and graspable thing.

To be crystal clear about the nature of reality is to have complete mastery over phenomenal appearances. Without complete understanding of the nature of existence, not only is there no mastery over data, there is a bouncing around between all the internal and external data with you as the pivot point.

The personal identity that you take yourself to be doesn't need any kind of examination or correction. Simply rely on open intelligence for a short moment—that's your true identity. There has never been a person who needs to be handled or taken care of.

There isn't a single datum that has ever had independent existence, so what does that say about the "you" that you're trying to fix up? Would you try to reshape space to make it into a better space? No, space is always *as it is*, and this is the nature of open intelligence as well—open intelligence is always *as it is*. It's never made into a subject; it's never made into an object. Wherever subject and object are seen, open intelligence is looking from within that subject and object. There's never any separation or division anywhere. Be very clear about this.

Even though open intelligence is completely obvious and undeniable, it often goes unrecognized, but it won't continue to go unrecognized for long. There are many people now who are instinctively recognizing open intelligence and who are applying that recognition in their lives and in collective problem-solving. These early pioneers are innovators, and their innovation will create a groundswell within humankind that will carry others towards recognizing the basic state. People will see the benefits of what the innovators are doing, and they will want to apply what they have seen to their own lives and to the problems they are trying to solve.

There are countless problems that need to be solved and countless problems we've been unable to solve. People everywhere are interested in what methods will actually be of benefit in terms of solving those problems, and they will only give up on a method when it shows itself to be unworkable for them. However, when a method is found that provides beneficial solutions for long term problems, people will want to support and sustain that method, because they see the positive results that it brings.

RELAXED, INNOVATIVE AND OPEN THINKING

We have many kinds of metaphors that point to the complete openness of the basic state. The Internet is one possible example that comes to mind. The Internet as a whole came about through looking at things in an extremely open way. Extraordinary innovations like Google, Wikipedia and open source software point to a vantage that is wide open. The relaxed, innovative and open thinking that allows all kinds of new ideas to come about is the permanent reality of our own being. It's not just some random insight that pops through now and again in the IT world.

Have you noticed how fluid a person's identity can be on the Internet? People can create many different identities online, and they are no longer fixed to one personal identity. I wouldn't suggest doing this necessarily, but it does show us how fluid identity can be. This is one example that shows how our personal identity is a fiction; it doesn't really mean anything. We don't have to persist in a make-believe existence.

All appearances within us or outside us and our own appearance as a personal identity are like a mirage or a hologram. Just as we wouldn't seek anything in a hologram or a mirage to give us satisfaction or fulfillment, why should we seek anything in appearances? They are all vivid appearances of open intelligence and nothing else.

We're living in an era where all of humankind is connected in a global human culture. We are able to transport ourselves easily over long distances and communicate with each other through all kinds of extraordinary technological systems. For the first time in all of human history we have this ease of access to one another. It's very important for us to recognize this global connectivity, because our recognition of ourselves as a global human culture needs to inform and influence the way the world develops in coming generations.

We are presently going through a tremendous shift in the way we look at things. Rather than just seeing things in a superficial way and being limited to seeing everything as a cause that leads to an effect, we're capable of looking at things in a much broader way. In all areas of inquiry—whether it be religion or spirituality, philosophy, physics, mathematics, Internet technology or other kinds of technology—we are capable of really stretching ourselves to go beyond our preconceived limits.

In getting acquainted with the foundation of human experience, we get acquainted with the ground of being, and as we get familiar with that ground of being we have greater evidence and demonstration of who we really are as human beings. From that vantage we can see everything that occurs within that ground of being in a fresh and clear way.

When we get acquainted with this very far-reaching perspective, we become real pioneers. While there have always been pioneers in each generation, for the first time in human history we have a way of all of global human culture being able to directly access the ground of being so that many pioneers can emerge.

This is a very important shift that we're undergoing, and while it can be related to the experiences of many historical figures, it's not attached to any specific historical figure. There is no need to create a dogma or a world religion or anything of that kind. People are interested in the definitive experience of what it means to be human, and many are growing familiar with what that is. As we do this together as a global human culture, we can really address not only our own individual issues and concerns but also the issues and concerns of our families, communities and the world.

OPTIMAL ORGANIZATIONS

I have been very involved in community life and different kinds of social organizing from the time I was a teenager, but unfortunately what I found was that all the social organizations to which I was exposed were overwhelmed by the data of the people involved. The organizations were not able to get much done that was really beneficial to people.

When we've set the bar so low, then it's kind of hard to know what's above the bar! We as individuals must become totally clear: the best way for human society to socially organize is through the open intelligence of the individual members of human society. It can't come about in any other way. Until now we have not been very good at putting together social organizations that are optimal—whether they're businesses, corporations, governments, non-profits or whatever kind of organization it might be. There is a way to put together an organization that's optimal, but it requires that people stop being involved in sub-optimal ways of thinking and organizing.

Sub-optimal circumstances are everywhere, and we can continue to be involved in things like that or not. However, if there's an organization that has total clarity, where everyone's happy and really aspiring to be of maximum benefit, then those are the kinds of organizations we need to be part of, rather than continuing to carry on in some kind of sub-optimal condition.

There is perfectibility that's possible in the human condition, and that perfectibility is not wishful thinking; it is naturally present as a physical law of our own basic state. We have to instinctively realize that we are essentially that basic state ourselves and then form our organizations based on that realization.

KNOWLEDGE THAT BRINGS WELL-BEING

CHAPTER THREE

THE INTELLIGENCE OF NATURE

Great emphasis is placed today on diversity of opinion and ideas—everyone having their own data streams and then trying to build consensus from data-driven intelligence. However, we have been trying to build consensus out of diversity of data for hundreds of years, and it has only led to greater and greater incoherence.

It may seem helpful to try to build consensus amidst divergent views, but this methodology is in fact backward and anachronistic. We really need to be focusing on ways of training people to lead, innovate and create using methods of collaboration that are not based on data at all. The emphasis should no longer be on relying on one's narrow data or on self-promotion and furthering one's own agenda, but on open intelligence and the mutual success and benefit of all.

If a person is locked into a system, then the methods and goals the person is interested in will be based on that system alone. Even though they may have great ideas about all kinds of things, their thinking is so ingrained in the system that they will keep referencing everything back to this system—rather than setting aside all systems.

What is needed is the courage and insight to challenge the authority of knowledge. For people living in this time as well as in future generations, we want to have a form of knowledge that isn't constantly referring back to past knowledge in order to verify itself. We cannot continue trusting in the authority of past knowledge and acting according to it.

The young people today are questioning that past knowledge more and more, but in another way they're going along with it. For the young people today, as well as for *all* people today, discovering the nature of our own existence is a most worthwhile endeavor—rather than continuing to hold to systems of knowledge that haven't worked.

Young people have more of a carefree attitude and are really contributing a great deal. Many of them are becoming interested in being a part of a interconnected group rather than remaining separate as disconnected individuals; they are very interested in the benefit of the whole and having the world be a place for everyone to live together peacefully.

At the same time there can be a certain lack of seriousness that really is required at this pivotal point. Even though we can be carefree, in order to innovate and lead, we need to also be totally serious and clear. This requires standing up and saying, "No, I strongly disagree with what is going on, and I want to find a method that we can use that does not repeat the mistakes of the past."

The power of open intelligence is so immense, but it doesn't seem immense when it's bogged down in particularized systems of thought. The immense power of the intellect that is present in open intelligence has complete mastery over all data. This intelligence is the intelligence of nature—completely clear, stable and laser-like.

This intelligence of nature—our basic knowledge— understands that all knowledge is present all at once, that there is never any knowledge that is discovered or invented; it's just recognized as being already present. Usually we think of inventions and discoveries as something completely new, but all knowledge is already present in *one* time—non-dimensional and zero-less.

We'll never be able to make sense of the nature of existence by rearranging the same old puzzle pieces. We want to be clear about what is unworkable and look for what is workable, and above all we have to be questioning all authorities of knowledge. In order to really question what authorities of knowledge are saying, we first have to have instinctive recognition of open intelligence, and that can only come about in our own experience. When we have full recognition of open intelligence, we can hear any authority of knowledge and recognize whether it is spot-on or in grievous error.

SEEING THINGS IN A NEW WAY

When we don't know how to connect with the simplicity of the natural presence of our experience, then we scamper about lost in a conventional way of thinking. Most of us never have access to any kind of knowledge that will jolt us out of our arrogance and ignorance.

There are some interesting examples in the past of how humankind has completely misperceived reality. A common belief many years ago was that the earth was flat and that if a ship sailed too far it would fall off the edge. However, some people believed that the earth wasn't flat, and they proved it by traveling across the oceans without falling off the edge. The people who thought the earth wasn't flat developed this new notion, then slowly gathered a few supporters and then proved that their idea was true. Yet, it took some time for their discovery to become common knowledge.

In a similar way, we have fundamental misperceptions about our own reality. Humankind has been very focused on appearances, and descriptive frameworks have been developed and believed in which describe a dualistic reality based on good and bad. The premise is that there are positive and negative things that occur, and the more we have of the positive, the less we'll have of the negative, and vice versa.

Even though we've assumed this and deeply believed in it, it has in fact never been the case. We've never been able to eradicate the negative by accumulating the positive—not within each of us as individuals or within society in general. When we really understand how we've misled ourselves in the past, then maybe we can say to ourselves, "Well, if we've misled ourselves so grossly in the past, perhaps we're misleading ourselves now, too. Is this assumption about good and bad one of the ways we are misleading ourselves?"

When we don't accurately perceive our reality, then we live a life based on confusion. We really don't understand ourselves, and we don't fully understand much of what is going on. We fail to see the very simple nature of reality, because we have relied on descriptions to determine what we're experiencing. By relying on descriptions rather than on our actual instinctive experience of reality, we are always looking for a new description to replace the description we are currently having. We're always caught up in our data, and we overlook the basic state of everything just *as it is*.

The basic state is beyond all phenomenal appearances. As data are only expressions of the basic state itself, they have no independent or individual substantiality, identity or existence other than the basic state. When phenomena are reduced to their fundamental essence, there's only the basic state and nothing else. As long as we don't see that everything rests within a basic state, we can never go beyond our self-limiting ideas about who we are and what the world is.

INSTINCTIVE COMPREHENSION

In Balanced View we talk about "open intelligence and data." Most of us learn to focus on data and rearrange them in order to have a good life. We never learn anything about open intelligence, which is the fundamental intelligence, the balanced view in which all the data appear. We never learn there is something about us that is profound and which has mastery over all the data. Reliance on that view rather than on data provides for a fundamental intelligence that is entirely clear.

By the power of open intelligence, an exponential type of intelligence opens up. We're able to see all kinds of things about our knowledge tools that we've never seen before. We're able to take our specialized field of knowledge to exponential heights of benefit. We don't become wrapped up in our knowledge as a way of identifying ourselves as someone special; rather, our knowledge is directed towards the benefit of all. We see ways to benefit ourselves and all of human society that we couldn't possibly have seen by relying on data.

No matter what kind of method we're trying—environmentalism, political activism, spirituality, science—there are many data associated with all of them. By the power of open intelligence, one is able to subsume all data in a fundamental intelligence, rather than clinging to fixed ideas of what science is, what philosophy is or what spirituality and religion are.

Even though we've made great advances in human society, we've also created a precipitous environment for ourselves. We continue to hold to actions based on points of view that could lead to the extinction of the human race. Without the clarity of open intelligence, actions can be taken in a blind fashion—such as dumping pollutants into the air and water or spreading them over the earth. However, from open intelligence, it becomes impossible to take such action, because all actions are naturally of benefit to all. We sustain our own selves in a beneficial way, and by learning directly from that experience we're able to benefit others.

There's an immediate seeing—a sort of forecast scenario—of exactly how any kind of action would turn out. This comes about not in a thought-driven way, but in a deeply instinctive way. There is a knowing about what to do and what not to do, knowing how to act and when to act, and this is natural to everyone.

We human beings are an expression of an intelligent process that can understand the nature of all of reality. One could say that our responsibility is to instinctively comprehend our role in nature, and by the power of open intelligence we can do that.

BASIC KNOWLEDGE

The basic state is the only source of well-being. You could have all the knowledge in the world about every single phenomenon—what it's made of and everything about its functions according to the most advanced forms of physics, mathematics and analysis—and you still wouldn't have well-being. Well-being can only come from knowledge of the basic state.

The basic knowledge of who you are is absolutely lucid, unobstructed and clear, yet it can go unrecognized if you are not alert to its presence. The only way to have that basic knowledge is to instinctively bring it to everything you do. When you bring basic knowledge to your experience, living life becomes effortless; otherwise, life is a lot of work.

It's not possible to use dualistic language systems to describe something that is beyond description. This is why the instinctive recognition of open intelligence is so important; unless there is the instinctive recognition in relation to one's *own experience*, it is impossible to gain access to open intelligence. If someone was introduced to the *idea* of open intelligence but had not applied it in a thoroughgoing fashion to all of their experiential understanding of their own life, there would be no way for them to ever be able to describe it in a way that would really ring true.

Open intelligence can never be adequately described in the scholarly or academic language that currently exists today, because that kind of language can never awaken the instinctive recognition of open intelligence. The spontaneous self-release of the here-and-now can never be captured by description. It is a song that needs to be sung in a certain way, and when the song is sung in that certain way, then *boom*, people can get it easily. What greater adventure could there possibly be than to hear the song of what is really true about yourself ringing within you in an undeniable way?

A COMMON LANGUAGE

For the first time in history human society is a global community, and it is important to see what would be of most benefit in the most effective and practical way for the people of the world. We want to see how we can solve the hideous problems we've created. We also want to further strengthen the great things we have come up with to meet the challenges we face.

This can best come about through using a common language that is utilizable worldwide. "A common language" does not have to do with a widely spoken language like English being the one language that people use to communicate with one another; rather, the language that is being described here has to do with the ideas, vocabulary, examples and insights that are understandable to the most people, regardless of what national language is being used. Whether this common language is used between individuals or in organizations and communities, it has to be a language that people everywhere can understand. This universality of language will be a springboard for great benefit in an all-inclusive way.

A great deal of effort has been made towards discovering what works in this regard. Trainings have been developed that forward the idea of open intelligence for everyone all over the world, and the trainings have been made commonly available in a language that can be easily grasped by many, many people.

Tools have been developed for people who would benefit from using them, and it has become clear with experience that the tools work everywhere. So, a committed group of people can make themselves available, and they can completely serve whoever naturally comes forward and wants to adopt what's already working.

A lot of this grew up out of people's experience in dealing individually with their own data. They came to see that skillfully dealing with data is not a spiritual or religious matter. It can be called that, but more basically, it's a *human* matter. The actual context is that of human nature and the optimal human condition, which is a much broader context than the spiritual or religious perspective alone. As soon as open intelligence is put into a fixed category—such as spiritual or religious—fewer people may be interested in it.

When we find something within human nature that is a source of complete relief, then it's important to draw on that. What human society needs is that which is of immediate benefit to many, many people—not just a few.

RELAXING WITH COMPELLING THOUGHTS

As everything is allowed to be at rest in the basic state, the open intelligence that is inseparable from the basic state becomes more and more obvious at all times. But what does that look like exactly?

Let's say that you have a thought and then that leads to another thought, which itself leads to yet another thought. For example, you think, "Oh, look at that attractive person!" and that's the first thought. Then the next thought is, "Oh, maybe that person would like me?" Then comes the thought, "Is it possible that we could be together?" Pretty soon we start to imagine being together with that person and the emotions and sensations associated with that. Through this process, we develop a whole descriptive framework that follows from the initial thought of attraction.

If we are practicing short moments of open intelligence, repeated many times, when that initial thought comes up, we can relax completely and allow the thought to disappear like a line drawn in water. When we see that the thought disappears in and of itself, we see that each thought is free in its own place in a open intelligence that is not limited to or identified with an individual. It is an instinctive open intelligence that appears within the basic state and is inseparable from it. The basic state is the basis of every single phenomenon.

UNFLINCHING IN THE FACE OF DATA

We can never be unaffected by external data unless we are first unaffected by our own internal data. There is a wonderful word we can use to describe how it is to be totally unaffected by data, and that word is "unflinching." The word means that we are courageously unmoved and unafraid in facing anything that we experience. So, by being unflinching in the face of our own data—without trying to change them into something else—we will see that we're not affected by anyone else's data either.

This is a huge shift because we spend all of our lives reacting to our internal data and to the external data of people, places and things. When we are unflinching in the face of our own internal data, we become unflinching in the face of external data, no matter what they are.

The fruit of our own experience is what teaches us this. It's when we simply stop; we put our foot on the brake and say, "I'm just not going to let myself be scared and confused anymore. I'm not going to allow myself to live in a terror that is of my own making." Part of that is admitting that the terror *is* of our own making.

No matter what age we are, when we commit to our unflinching nature, we give ourselves the greatest gift. That open intelligence and unflinching nature is the basis from which we want to live. It's the only basis by which we can make breakthroughs that help deal with the dilemma the world is in.

From our fundamental state of open intelligence, no matter what is going on inside us or around us, we do not see it in the same way we did before. No matter how gut-wrenching the emotions, no matter how plaguing the thoughts, no matter how overwhelming the bodily sensations, no matter how extreme the horror of reactivity to what's occurring globally, we cannot see it in the way we did before.

If we have the perspective of clarity, we can immediately see what isn't working in all the current forms of inquiry, organizations and knowledge, and we're not fooled by anything. No matter how commanding the voice of conventional authority may be, we are not fooled, and it is increasingly this way. Through clearly seeing the nature of our own data we begin to have tremendous clarity about everything that is going on. We can see what is going on in the people, places or things we encounter. It doesn't mean that we're spouting off about our ability to do so, but it means that we have the decisive recognition of open intelligence to act in a wise and beneficial manner.

If we are not unflinching, we'll be going right along with the way everybody else thinks about everything. We won't be able to see that we can create fields of knowledge that have never been created before. Unless we're unflinching in the face of all data, we can never see that we can go beyond all current knowledge, whether it's in music, science, mathematics or whatever it is. When we're unflinching in the direct encounter with all of our own data, we see that we rest in the basic knowledge of the way things are.

"Being unflinching" doesn't mean that our experience will look a certain way. It doesn't mean that every little thing we see or come into contact with is going to look rosy and beautiful. It means that whatever our experience is, it shines with brilliant open intelligence and we're unflinching in the direct encounter with it. We don't see ourselves as vulnerable or controlled by our experience any longer.

It's really important to take complete charge. You are what you are. No one can give your true nature to you and no one can take it away from you, but you can be sure that there are people who can help you be unflinching in your own experience of it.

THE ULTIMATE SATISFACTION

A lot of people seem to be happy in the surreal wasteland of data, and that's just the way it is. We once tried to convince ourselves we were happy there, too! Once we decide that something is going to make us happy, we take that up and we spend a lot of time gritting our teeth and saying, "This is making me happy, I know it is!" All the while we are wailing inside thinking, "Get me out of here!"

At every turn there is some kind of seductive influence to lure us into thinking that *this time* a datum is going to make us happy. As we gain more certainty in open intelligence, we see that this isn't the case, and we are just not willing to go there anymore. We know that no matter how seductive the data might be, there really isn't anything there. When we rest as the pure space of all these seductive influences, then we can really come to know ourselves to be beyond seduction and entertainment. What is more important: to chase after yet another alluring fantasy, or to gain familiarity and certainty in that which is totally substantial in its insubstantiality?

By gaining certainty in open intelligence when we are young we save ourselves from a lifetime of being seduced by things that cannot provide any satisfaction. The things we might think are going to give some kind of satisfaction—intimate relationships, having children, developing careers—are not sources of ultimate satisfaction. We may have tried to make ourselves believe that they were bringing us ultimate satisfaction, but after gaining certainty in open intelligence we see these things for what they are.

ETHICAL SPONTANEITY

What are ethics? Ethics are our moral system turned outwards; they are the way our inner moral system appears in our behavior. Most people think that cultivating one's character in a positive way is the epitome of what a human being can be, but it isn't. The epitome of what a human being can be is natural perfection, and the recognition of that natural perfection leads to an ethical spontaneity that no acquired system of ethics or morality can provide.

What greater moral and ethical system could we have than the moral and ethical system of open intelligence, which allows us to be of benefit in all of our activities? We have profound insight into everyone we meet, and this is the basis of true compassion, of true connection and of a human society that is really profound and great. All of this comes from gaining certainty in open intelligence.

Our parents, schools and churches might teach us the difference between right and wrong, but if we only know those ideals, we'll always be living in a world of differences. There

33

are very few people who can ever live up to those ideals; however, by gaining certainty in open intelligence we can discover the basis of spontaneous morality and ethics. This is a much better way to go.

Some of the people who have received the Great Freedom/Balanced View Training are in prison or even on death row. There is an incredible proliferation of data associated with being in prison, but many of these men are very ripe for gaining certainty in open intelligence, because they can no longer take advantage of most of the antidotes they had in their life before prison. Their previous world of antidotes has ceased to exist, including the antidote of criminal activity—if in fact that's what they've done—so many of them are very quick to take to the Great Freedom/Balanced View Training.

Many say, "Wow, I'm in prison, but I've never felt so free." No amount of ethical trainings ever stopped them from doing what they did or allowed them to really understand their behavior, but now they've naturally found that ethical and moral impulse within themselves. Only certainty in the open intelligence can help any of us understand why we do what we do. Whether we're on death row in a maximum security prison or we're running around freely in the world, we have to have open intelligence to be able to understand why we do what we do.

OPEN INTELLIGENCE IN SLEEP AND DREAMS

Most of us haven't really thought too much about dreams and sleep. We feel that when we go to sleep we're not really consciously present at all, and when we are dreaming all kinds of things happen and we have no control over them whatsoever. However, by gaining certainty in open intelligence all of our data—whether they are in waking, dreaming or sleeping—come to our assistance in seeing things as they truly are.

When data—including those of our own body and mind—appear in dreams, they seem to be real and independently existing, but they are not. Maybe in one dream we've gone through some horrendous experience, but in another dream we have something great happen; however, whether it's a negative dream or a positive dream, they're equally insubstantial. That is such a great teaching that leads us to see our daytime appearances with much more discernment.

Birth, life, death, waking, dreaming and sleeping are a continuum of open intelligence. The more we instinctively recognize open intelligence, the more this will be clear to us, and the more we will have the same kind of understanding about our daytime experiences that we have about our dreams.

A way to be introduced to this understanding is to maintain open intelligence when you go to sleep. As you fall asleep, notice that the data become more subtle. They pass into a condition that is more dreamlike, even though you are superficially awake. You can still identify yourself as being awake even though there are sequences of data that are phantasmagoric. What you have identified as your body and mind are sleeping in your bed, but open intelligence is still wide awake, vivid and alert. That is particularly convincing, because most of us have felt very powerless in the face of dreams and sleep.

Instead of getting wrapped up in describing the subtle data or the phantasmagoric images that occur in a dream, the focus is on maintaining open intelligence. At that point there is only lucid open intelligence without anything else. You might recognize that you are asleep, and there might be some images appearing, but you can recognize that, even though you are asleep, you're aware. Open intelligence is aware of sleeping and of dreams. You as a sleeper and dreamer are the self-manifestation of open intelligence.

This experience you have at night is also extremely convincing in terms of the data you have during the day. You have now transmuted these two states of sleep and dreams into their true clarity-nature of open intelligence. With this insight you won't feel so affected by the data that occur during the day.

It is important to recognize that this practice is not necessary for gaining certainty in open intelligence. It's a very convincing and authoritative practice, but it's nothing to get all wrapped up in. What's most important is to identify open intelligence as your bare state of naturalness all the time.

Section Two
The Gifts of Open Intelligence

FREE OF UPS AND DOWNS

CHAPTER FOUR

RECOGNIZING YOUR TRUE NATURE

All appearances are appearances of sheer delight. I would really be a ridiculous person if I said something like that and didn't have my own direct experience to back it up. For twenty-eight years I have had the great privilege to live this way, and I have gone through all kinds of things in life. I have had people born and people die, I have had serious illnesses, undergone major surgeries, nearly died, had all kinds of ups and downs financially and all the many different types of occurrences in life that anyone can have. Yet, my life is a life of sheer delight.

It is so clear to me that the super-radiance of open intelligence illuminates everything. How did I come to know that this is true? I made a decision at one point that I was sick and tired of being sick and tired! I was sick and tired of being on a roller coaster ride all the time. Once I clearly saw that the things I had learned in life weren't working, it was easy for me to get off the roller coaster.

When I was a young woman I had something happen in my life that was violent and unexpected. I was in great danger, and I could have lost my life. I was able to get out of that situation alive, but I was left totally traumatized and with incredible paranoia, terror, bewilderment and horror. Wherever I turned, I could find no relief. None of my philosophical, spiritual, religious and psychological assumptions could help me find my way out.

When I talked to people about what was going on, they would say, "This is extremely difficult, but this too shall pass." I thought that meant that it would get better, but it didn't—it got worse. I just couldn't find any way out of this maelstrom of intense thoughts and emotions. They were so evident in every single moment of my experience, and they were like an onslaught that couldn't be stopped. I felt hopeless and powerless. There wasn't any relief anywhere—not even in ordinary things like eating a cake, having a martini, smoking marijuana or anything else. None of the strategies for relaxation or diversion were of any use whatsoever.

But then suddenly—within all the total terror and upset—I realized that all of these thoughts and emotions had the same underlying basis. I also realized that this underlying basis was one of complete relief. I could see that I had a choice of either getting worked up by whatever was going on or relaxing and enjoying the ride. I saw that open intelligence was the essence of all these appearances. No matter what these appearances were, they were fed by open intelligence, which is the essence and basis of whatever appears. I hadn't known before that there was anything like complete relief, but now I simply enjoyed the relief I felt and allowed the thoughts and emotions to do their own thing.

As I relaxed into the vast unknowable expanse that is the natural order of everything, I found that there is a clarity and an intelligence that are beyond all the turmoil of thoughts and emotions. In that is an immense power and force of creativity. This is something that is utterly indescribable. The more that I allowed this great relief to be the case, the freer I felt.

I had always been driven to be a good person, but I didn't feel that I had ever been able to achieve that goodness in my life. However, in this relief and rest there was a naturally occurring compassion and an ability to sense, feel and see like never before. There was a goodness that was emanating naturally. That was amazing to me.

This amazing insight was something that appeared in my mind stream in a completely natural way, and I knew that this relief was available to everyone. It was clear to me that there was no turning back from this relief that I had found, even though this was something I had never heard about from anyone else.

I found myself suddenly being able to do all kinds of things that I've never been able to do before. I could create at an entirely new level that hadn't been available to me at all. I didn't even know it was there before, because I had been completely blind to it. This became very interesting and compelling to me, and there was nothing else I wanted to know about.

Relying on that open intelligence allowed me to be more creative in a very practical way in my own life. No longer was I ruled by my thoughts and emotions. They became less and less significant to me, and they were no longer the information that I relied on. I found that I was capable of contributing and understanding things on an entirely new level that was completely beyond conventional constraints.

From then on, with every single book I picked up, I could completely analyze and understand everything that was in it. I could see exactly—clear as the light of day—how the data came about in the author, and I could see how the conclusions in the book would play out. This was something I had not been able to see before.

It was very clear to me that there was incredible authority in what I had discovered. I kept relying on open intelligence, and after a while the open intelligence was obvious all the time, and I didn't need to try to rely on it anymore. What had always been there in the background without being noticed was now being acknowledged in every moment. Once it was acknowledged and then re-acknowledged repeatedly and diligently again and again, it became an obvious reality.

In this way I came to see that all descriptions are essentially equal, because their essence is open intelligence. If I'd tried to understand all these descriptions and decide how they all fit together, then I would have been lost in a tailspin of descriptions forever. I chose instead to rely on open intelligence. No matter how much solace my status, reputation or material and social circumstances had brought me, they were of no comfort any longer. I had no desire whatsoever to try and manufacture meaning out of them. I had given up on that, and I didn't want it anymore.

All my questions about intelligence, life and self were definitively answered in a single moment. It was as if every thought, emotion and experience I had ever had in my life passed through my mind stream in a single instant, and I could see they all had the same essence. I became convinced that there was a way of living that didn't involve being ruled by thoughts and emotions. I also saw that anyone who chose that timeless way of living would be able to see that everything came out of their own awareness. Truly, in the relaxed naturalness of being, everything is a sheer delight!

DON'T WORRY, BE HAPPY

There are two maxims to live by: either "worry and don't be happy" or "don't worry and be happy." We have gotten into the mess of point of view by believing so much that the data are real and that they have some kind of power to affect how we feel. No matter what we have believed, we can just step back, relax and see what is really going on. From that clear vantage, it's a lot easier to really understand the nature of our life. We can also create a powerful life where we can be of benefit to ourselves and others.

The spontaneous, naturally occurring, self-perfected reality can't be refined in any way. The whole idea that it can be refined, corrected, analyzed or indulged is simply another point of view. Why throw more data into the mix? Just relax and know that nothing need be done.

As you relax, you will have a much clearer understanding of how to live a human life. No matter how much you believe in needing to correct or comment on what appears, rely on open intelligence instead. If for instance fear arises, you might think, "If I don't do something about this fear, something bad might happen. If I don't have a way to understand this, maybe it won't work out the way I want it to work out." Rather than going with that story, you maintain open intelligence as the fear comes to full fruition. The movement of fear comes to full potential as the dynamic energy of open intelligence, but once you allow it to come to full potential, *boom*, spontaneously it vanishes without a trace like a line drawn in water or like the flight path of a bird in the sky. Then you start to be able to see the obviousness of open intelligence in all situations. It won't happen though if you shut down at any point in that process or if you are lost in your stories.

By relying on open intelligence the story is stopped short, and the tension that would normally be poured into the story disappears in and of itself. The more restful you become, the less impulse there is to take up any story. You see that no story is worth having when you compare it to the benefits of open intelligence. It's just a very simple choice: "Do I want to be happy, or do I want to be worried?" We make that choice to be happy by releasing the tension of belief in data.

ULTIMATE HUMILITY

Humility is not a state of weakness—it is a place of strength. The natural humility of open intelligence is not a matter of inferiority, resignation or submission. We accept ourselves as we are, including all our data. In this way all situations can be utilized to intensify the recognition of open intelligence. Allowing everything to be *as it is* without needing to compulsively create a reality is what true humility is. We let everything be self-perfected as it fundamentally is and utilize all the means that are available for doing that.

When we are humble, we are totally willing to accept help, knowing that without it we cannot progress further. Even though we may imagine that we are special, we're in fact fundamentally just like everyone else and really quite simple in our essence. A humorous way to describe ourselves would be as simpletons! We are exalted as wisdom beings, but we are exalted in our simple-ness. We do not become exalted by becoming rich, famous, admired or by being better than others. Being totally simple—that's the way to go. It's good to be a simpleton, it really is!

We just relax, and in being a simpleton we find our true power. Being a simpleton means that we are allowing ourselves to be naked with all of our data. It might be a little scary at first, but by the power of short moments, the data quickly lose their power to scare us.

We want that kind of maturity, because it will sustain us for the rest of our lives. It's only when we allow everything to be *as it is* that we're truly able to be free of everything, and then we're really able to connect intimately with everyone and everything. If we don't get real with all of our own data exactly as they are, then we won't be able to understand other people or be connected with them in any real way.

To live our lives based on data is humiliation, but to be absolutely real with everything as it is about ourselves is ultimate humility. This really is the ultimate humility. In this ultimate humility we connect ourselves with everything that is.

LIFE WITHOUT UPS AND DOWNS

Life without ups and downs is inconceivable to most people. Yet, life without ups and downs is the natural condition of every human being. Ups and downs are all based on believing that thoughts, emotions, sensations and other experiences have the power to cause ups and downs, but that is a fundamental misunderstanding. What appears within open intelligence never affects open intelligence in any way. No matter what appears, open intelligence is unwavering and unaltered.

If you can acknowledge open intelligence more and more, you will come to know who you truly are. You will be able to handle all situations without impediment, and you will be able to do things you could never have imagined doing or achieving. This will occur for you naturally and effortlessly by simply letting the powerful current of open intelligence be *as it is* with no need to impose descriptions upon it.

What is really required is taking a stand. You want to ensure yourself a state of mind that will not be subjected to ups and downs based on personal or world events. It is important that you ensure yourself this, because the super-intelligence that comes from complete mental and emotional stability will allow you to deal skillfully with all your circumstances. Through deep insight, clarity and compassion you will know how best to contribute to the world in a beneficial way.

You have to have confidence in the path you are on. If you were walking along a footpath and you saw that the path would take you exactly where you wanted to go, then if you stumbled over a rock on the way you would keep going anyway. You wouldn't say, "Oh, this rock is evidence that this path leads nowhere." Keep your eye on the prize. If you are on a path and you are certain that it leads you to where you want to go, then if you stumble on something along the way, you need not be deterred.

We could be in an abusive relationship that was emotionally or physically violent; we could be living in a world that is war torn and fraught with terrorism; we could be in a workplace that is unsatisfying and in which we never feel any fulfillment, a job where we feel trapped where we feel we have to be there in order to make money, and all of these could be ways of seeing ourselves as incapable, disempowered victims who were incapable of anything better—or not.

When we rely on our own empowered nature, it becomes obvious in us and in all our actions. When a person is empowered and enlivened by being in touch with their own open intelligence, they do not have to say a word—one could just look and see the clarity present in them. They walk in the room and it is like, *whoosh,* what happened! And what do we see? We see what is most fundamental in ourselves when we see someone like that.

The qualities and activities of life that flow from mental and emotional stability are exceptionally powerful. They are powerful beyond the greatest powers that we see presently demonstrated in politics, business, technology or other areas of human endeavor. These are the kind of powers that are earth-shattering, that really change the way people think and live for the better on a very large scale. If we want to recognize those powers within ourselves, we cannot be a victim any longer. All of our ideas of being a victim of ourselves or of other people, places and things just have to go out the window.

BE GENTLE WITH YOURSELF

Open intelligence is only found in accepting your data exactly as they are with no need to try to be somebody else. In whichever way your particular data appear, that's just the way it is. There's nothing to be made out of them. Accept yourself the way you are; you're all you've got!

When there is some kind of breakdown—huge or small—within ourselves or with someone else, it's important to be gentle. In the same way that you lift yourself up when you choose to take advantage of open intelligence rather than data, you can also lift others. By being gentle with yourself and relying on open intelligence, you can be there to lift others up again and again, just as you would lift yourself up.

You become compassionate because you have seen that you're like everyone else. Rather than trying to make yourself into some kind of paragon of virtue, you see how you have suffered from indulging in your data and how others have done the same.

You give up all of your strategies, and you see yourself exactly as you are. This is how the most compassionate, loving people on earth have become that way: by seeing themselves exactly as they are. That's where compassion arises. You have to be able to reach that point where you realize that everything is the self-reflection of open intelligence.

THE GREATEST DISCOVERY

When I was a young woman I had much success initially, but I was never comforted by that success. I thought, "Wow, this is really scary, because I have all these great things happening, but I actually feel less mental stability as a result." I could see this in myself and it didn't feel good.

Throughout my twenties I was working in a university where I met many accomplished people, and I was able to get to know them and talk to them about their lives and their ideas. They were writing all these wonderful books, but from the things I'd hear about them or the kinds of relationships they had with people, including me, I could see that they really didn't know what was going on. That too was very scary to me because I thought, "These are the people you are supposed to be able to look to for answers, but they don't actually have the answers."

Not only did I lose faith in the people that I had been listening to and looking to as authorities, but I lost faith in the methods they were using. I thought, "These methods didn't work for any of the people who have developed them, so how are they going to work for me?" I gave up my faith in popular psychological, psychiatric, religious, spiritual and philosophical methods. Even though I wasn't physically sick, I was in a dilemma much like many other people who are suffering. I wondered how I would be able to get through the rest of my life, and that thought was very frightening.

The more overwhelmed I felt by what was going on for me, the more desperate I felt, the more hopeless I felt, the more powerless I felt, and the more I felt I was a victim and that I needed someone to save me. "Somebody is supposed to take care of me and tell me how to do it."

The people that I met knew how to apply antidotes to situations; they knew how to either indulge thoughts, emotions, sensations or experiences, or avoid them or replace them with positive thoughts and emotions, but none of that worked for me. I felt dissatisfied while applying all those antidotes, and whether they were internal or external, the antidotes never led to any resolution of the dismay that I felt.

I reached a point where I did give up my right to be a victim of my thoughts, emotions, sensations and experiences—and that came in an instant! I suddenly saw that all of these ideas that I had about everything that were self-generated or that I had learned from others all arose in the basic space of open intelligence. I saw that in open intelligence all these ideas are all absolutely equal. That was amazing to me!

One after another I would check out all my data, and I would see that they all were alike in that they didn't really have any solid substance, and I couldn't really say that they were located anywhere. If I had a thought of, say, depression, it didn't seem to be located anywhere in particular. Furthermore, if I thought of myself as being an individual with a fixed identity, that thought was no different from the thought of depression or the thought of love. All these thoughts about everything, no matter what they were, were equal.

I explored that equality more and more in my own experience by relaxing my mind completely. I didn't really call that relaxation anything. I just knew that when I relaxed there was complete relief, and when I didn't need to have a story about everything that was going on, there was complete relief. Not only was there complete relief, but moment-to-moment there was increasing empowerment and enlivenment of something totally vital within me that I knew was going to carry me through. Not only did I feel completely empowered, I also felt kind. I felt kindness towards myself, and I felt a natural kindness and openness to other people.

Even if everyone in the world came up to me and said, "You don't know what you are talking about," it wouldn't have mattered. I realized that I had found whatever anyone might ever look for in life.

COMPLETE MENTAL AND EMOTIONAL STABILITY

The thought often comes up, "I need to fit in. I want to be accepted and acknowledged by people," but what are we trying to fit in to? We may have been trying to fit in with our family, with our friends, in our workplace, in our community and so on, but has being accepted by any of these groups ever given us complete mental and emotional stability?

We want to fit in and not be ostracized, so we conform to the norm to one degree or another. Even if we fight the norm and we become anti-authoritarian, that is just another extreme of conforming to the norm—believing in it enough to want to rebel against it.

If we try to shape ourselves to everything our family, friends, workplace or community expects of us, we'll be all tied up in knots and frustrated, because it is an endless task. The moment we think we've achieved everything everybody else wants of us, there will always be the next thing. So, why would we want to keep going that way?

Speculating about what other people are doing or thinking is very weakening, and trying to set things up so we'll be respected and liked—wow, it's exhausting just thinking about it! It's much more enjoyable to let things be as they are, and then pretty soon we find that everything has a sense of enjoyment and pleasure to it. Through that we see that we really have choices. We don't have to keep up the frenetic pace of shape-shifting ourselves into something based on opinions.

Know yourself, then whatever you need to be in relation to others will be absolutely clear. Be at ease and let everything rest in its natural place. You'll be changing the world just through the way you are living your own life. What a contribution!

OUR INHERENT HAPPINESS

Our naturally occurring inherent happiness has a lot more to tell us than any thought or emotion ever will. We are the ones that make ourselves unhappy by believing that our thoughts and emotions have something important to tell us, and we have to take responsibility for that. Even if we have deeply engrained thoughts and emotions—and a lot of us do—the only release from them is in open intelligence. Our inherent happiness is what we want to get familiar with—not with all the thoughts and emotions that seem to describe unhappiness.

Certainty in open intelligence becomes stronger than the thoughts and emotions themselves, and we see that the thoughts and emotions are simply the dynamic energy of that open intelligence.

One of the extreme ideas that many people have is, "Open intelligence can happen for other people, but it won't happen for me." But when that data stream appears, where does it appear? It appears in open intelligence. Whether it has to do with people who are conventionally described as being really virtuous and beautiful or those who are described as being totally nasty and horrible, *everyone* rests equally in the natural perfection of open intelligence.

Enjoying Life to the Fullest

CHAPTER FIVE

A LIFE OF ABUNDANCE, PEACE AND HAPPINESS

Early on in my life I had an idea of what was possible for everyone on earth, including myself. This idea was that people could be happy, kind, generous and peaceful and that they would have the things they needed: food, water, health care, education and sufficient income so that they could live life in a way that would be of benefit to themselves and others. It really comes down to very fundamental and practical ideas about how we want to live our life. What are we willing to do? Do we want to find a way to bring about real change?

I felt that, even if all my friends and family told me that what I was doing was crazy, that wouldn't change my intention. I was that clear within myself; no matter what anyone else thought, nothing would change my commitment to this vision. I had a deep abiding belief that there were many other people around the world who shared my vision. I saw what was possible, but I could have just had that dream and never done anything about it. However, over time I gradually became more committed to that vision.

First I had to bring about that vision in my own life; I couldn't simply run around telling everyone else how to do it. In order for it to have any authenticity with other people, I had to be able to bring that about in myself. Once I had brought that about in myself, then I felt that it was time to benefit others. At that point I was willing to let everything else go, and I had to find a life circumstance that would empower my ability to be of benefit. I knew as well that I had to do this while at the same time honoring all of my previous commitments and relationships.

If we want to have the friends we've always wanted to have, live in circumstances we've always wanted to live in and work in circumstances we've always wanted to work in, we have to make a commitment to that. We have to say, "This is what I'm going to do. This is what my life is now!" Period, exclamation point, with no more question mark. That's how it comes about—by making a commitment. Once you make that commitment, then the certainty starts to dawn in you that you made the right choice. But you have to make the commitment first.

THE TREMENDOUS LOVE, CLARITY AND ENERGY IN US

We have a choice about how we perceive things. If we see ourselves as victims of our thoughts, emotions, sensations and other experiences, then we'll live our life feeling victimized by ourselves as well as by other people. As we recognize short moments, many times, we see how we have made ourselves a victim of our data. No one did it to us, and no dramatic or traumatic event in itself can make us into victims. We were victims because we chose to be.

We will have no real well-being as long as we take ourselves to be a victim of what is happening to us. It's absolutely essential to come to the point where we can say, "Wow, to continue suffering from all of my miserable thoughts, feelings and experiences is unnecessary, and to have done so for so long was just a choice I was making."

We could continue to see ourselves as victims who are disempowered and incapable of anything better, but this is very sad. It's especially sad because human beings are innately powerful. The qualities and activities of life that flow from a stable mind are exceptionally powerful. They are powers that are earthshaking and which really can change the way people think and live on a very large scale.

Whereas the stance of the victim is one of powerlessness and helplessness, the stance of a person recognizing open intelligence as the basis of everything is one of tremendous power and helpfulness. We were looking for some relief when we sought refuge in being a victim of circumstances. But there is an intrinsic relief of tremendous love, clarity, energy and basic goodness that exists within us that need not be sought. It is found within us and within *all* our data. This is the most profound of all insights.

The only way to find that tremendous energy is by the power of allowing everything to be just *as it is* for short moments, many times. Short moments show us the way to the open door leading to our basic goodness, and by recognizing the tremendous power within us, that door is flung wide open.

THE POWER OF OUR LIFE

We're most skillful, most intelligent and most powerful simply by recognizing open intelligence. There's no one else to look to who can give us this treasure; it is to be found in ourselves and in our own experience.

There's no moment of experience that can be held onto or pushed away. There's only the spontaneous self-release of the here-and-now. We realize there's nothing to do; the short moments we take are just short moments of our already present peaceful nature. Eventually everything that we've thought ourselves to be is consumed by great, all-encompassing peace, love and serenity.

If we're willing to set all ideas aside and rely on short moments, then we are completely released from the need to be constantly trying to change things. We're able to allow experience to flow on by with no need to manipulate it in any way. We're able to allow all thoughts and emotions to flow on by with no need to regulate them or gain authority over them. We know through our own experience of short moments that all of the thoughts and emotions are instantaneously resolved without any effort.

If we're looking for a sign of accomplishment, here's a good one: we cheer up! We are released from obsessive self-involvement and the need to make our experience be anything other than what it is.

In short moments we truly come into the power of our life that we're meant to have. We want to use our skills to contribute to our family, to our community, to our nation and to the world, and by the power of short moments we are able to do that very decisively because our contribution comes from clarity. This is a power that can't be learned from a book or in school. It can only be found in our own experience.

A WONDERFUL LIFE

Your life can be everything you want it to be. Your life can be a circumstance of effortless living, effortless connection, effortless intimacy and effortless ease. Know that to be true. All of this comes about by short moments, repeated many times. It is a treasure trove of wish-fulfilling gems.

If we believe in all our thoughts, emotions, experiences and sensations—data—then we do not recognize open intelligence, and we will overlook this precious gem of inestimable value. This precious basis of everything fulfills all wishes. From the first moment of gaining certainty in open intelligence, we see that this is really something unique and special, and that is what attracts us again and again.

The more familiar we are with our identity as pure, unobstructed open intelligence, the more we're just entirely beneficial at all times without trying to do so. This doesn't require any effort; it's just a natural heartfelt impulse that is irrepressible and forever free flowing.

The more we rely on open intelligence, the easier our life will be in every respect. If we try to complicate our life with lots of other things, it will just be complicated with all those other things! Know that the training of short moments many times is always available. With a one hundred percent commitment it is guaranteed to become continuous at all times.

POWERFUL INTELLIGENCE

It is up to each one of us to see that our conduct is subsumed in the supreme conduct of open intelligence. When all conduct is subsumed in that supreme conduct of the instinctive recognition of open intelligence, then we live in a completely ethical and moral way without following any ethical or moral authority. This is the meta-morality or meta-ethic that is at the basis of everything.

Open intelligence supersedes the notions of good and bad, should and should not. Ideal conduct actually means to recognize that open intelligence is the basis of the flow of all perceptions. In a practical sense, rather than trying to behave in a certain way, we simply acknowledge open intelligence.

Conduct and the one who conducts it are inseparable. When we look for the one who engages in conduct or who refrains from conduct, neither is found anywhere. Our search for proper conduct is exhausted. Now we continue on in a relaxed way, nakedly seeing from within. We rely on open intelligence rather than trying to figure it all out based on data.

ULTIMATE HAPPINESS

If we look deeply into our own experience, we can see that the attainment of the things that many of us have sought—money, power, prestige, relationships—has never led to ultimate happiness. No matter how much we have of any of them, it has somehow never seemed to be exactly right. Even if we got the perfect job, the perfect car, the perfect partner, the perfect food, the perfect vacation, the perfect place to live, none of this would ensure our happiness.

We can see by simply looking around us that having all these things does not bring about complete happiness for people. What is more, there may be people who have none of those things who are bright and shining and totally happy. So, we can't say that any particular datum has anything to do with bringing about our ultimate happiness.

It may be that we're presently healthy, prosperous and secure, but our physical circumstances could change at any moment. This is true about our own physical body and all other circumstances in our lives. Not a single thing is permanent. Even if we did have all the things we desired, we know that at any moment they could all be snatched away. As a result, there is an underlying feeling of anxiety, because we know we can never trust completely in the things we acquire. We could continue to try to get more and more of them, but the underlying anxiety wouldn't leave us.

There is never a moment when all of our data will be set right—except in the total completeness of the here-and-now. True stability and confidence are found only in open intelligence, which is the basis of everything. The crystal clarity of what is spontaneously self-releasing and which can never be grasped, caught, or measured is what will give us the complete satisfaction we seek.

If we're feeling lost, confused and depressed, we need to rely on open intelligence alone. We rely on that which is seeing the confusion and loss. The confusion and what sees the confusion, the depression and what sees the depression, the lost-ness and what sees the lost-ness—all are inseparable. The seeing is equally in disturbance as it is in no-disturbance.

RELAX AND ENJOY LIFE

When we have done everything and we no longer need anything and there isn't anything whatsoever that can pull on us in any way, then we've come to absolute completeness.

When we stop for a moment and consider our life, how much of it has been spent running from one experience to another hoping to find some kind of comfort? For example, we get up in the morning, and let's say that we feel foggy or half-asleep, so we run for a cup of coffee or some other kind of pick-me-up to change what we feel. Then we look at the people around the breakfast table; we may start thinking about their shortcomings or why we don't want to be there with them at that moment—or we start feeling guilty because we've been thinking about their shortcomings and not wanting to be with them, and we try to relieve ourselves of that guilt by being nice to them.

Then we go to work, and we have to face the wild and wooly array of different personalities that we find there. We often feel powerless and helpless in the face of the challenges we have in the workplace. During the day we're thinking about some kind of pleasant state that we can get into that won't involve the state we're currently in, so we start thinking about what it will be like when we get off work. Then we're thinking about how nice it would be if we could retire!

At the end of the day we get off work, but things aren't yet what we hoped they would be, so we think, "I'll have a drink or a joint, or I'll watch TV or go to a movie or try out that new restaurant." Then, of course, there's always sex. Nothing else is working, so how about our old standby to provide a moment of complete relief? All the while we are seeking the next experience that will make us feel better. Yikes!

The very best thing we can do for ourselves is to live life with a one hundred percent commitment to open intelligence. Until we begin living as open intelligence, we will have so many expectations of how life needs to change. But when we have that commitment to open intelligence, less and less will we need to rely on trying to change things.

When the need to change ourselves and our circumstances is completely resolved and there is no longer a focus on a self-centered existence, then it's seen that the self-centered existence never was anything fixed or solid. By recognizing our natural beneficial being, the self-obsession that was once so prevalent is no longer to be found, and instead the desire to be of benefit in a very natural way pours forth.

Please relax and enjoy life. Don't beat yourself up with all the descriptions you've learned about what you need or what you need to be. When ideas come up: "Oh, I'm unemployed, I am employed; I am successful, I am not successful; I need to change this, I need to change that," relax and see that everything is *as it is* and that there is nothing to change.

INSTINCTIVE INTELLIGENCE

We can rely on the instinctive recognition of open intelligence, regardless of whether we describe ourselves as smart or stupid. Whatever our relative level of intelligence, we can give ourselves access to this instinctive intelligence that is beyond the labels of "smart" and "stupid." All the means we have for testing our conventional intelligence are based on data— temporary phenomena that we can never hold on to.

Why rely on a kind of intelligence that comes and goes? Why not rely on the permanent instinctive intelligence that is basic to us? In relying on that basic intelligence we'll have the smarts, so to speak, to handle everything that comes up no matter what stage of life we're in. Even if our intellectual capacities become duller as we get older, open intelligence will always be blazing. So, why rely on something that is limited and which will not take us through all of our life? Rely on that about us which will never change.

ACTING POWERFULLY IN THE WORLD

How do we learn to act powerfully in the world? Short moments, many times. Without that we will just be flying around with limited understanding, and we won't be able to help ourselves from having emotional reactions to situations that will lead us off in many directions. But if we just give ourselves some time to get grounded in the clarity of open intelligence and gain a confidence that is unshakable and unmovable, then we are going to be okay. We're not going to have to wonder what to do, because we'll always know what to do.

This doesn't mean that we are going to just walk around with a big smile on our face acting like some kind of sweetie-pie; no, wisdom can also be very wrathful. But there is a big difference between the wrathful compassion of open intelligence and getting angry, blowing your top, being out of control and saying anything you want. This type of response has no beneficial purpose; you hurt yourself and you hurt other people. Wrathful compassion is always motivated by love and wisdom, and the recipient, if they're receptive and open, will recognize that it's motivated by love and wisdom.

When you ground yourself in the clarity of open intelligence, you have an incredible power to see all kinds of things you couldn't see before. Think of it this way: you can see in all directions at once! You can see everything that's occurring, whether it's within your physical space or not, and you can also see how it's going to pan out. Open intelligence is timeless, so not only can you see what's occurring now, but you can also see how certain things will lead to other things if they continue to go that way.

From the clarity of open intelligence, you're no longer bound within conventional constructs. If you are an environmentalist, a doctor, an engineer, a bread baker or whatever you happen to be, you'll have an entirely different perspective when compared to a person without that insight—no matter how brilliant that person might be. From the perspective of clarity you will have a power that simply isn't present if there is no certainty in open intelligence.

Once there is no cage of conventional intellectual speculation about how to solve problems, then all kinds of new ways of looking at problems open up. If you have burning issues that are really important to you, then you want to act from the clarity that comes from certainty in open intelligence. You don't want to be acting based upon your data.

There's tremendous power in the practice of short moments, many times, because it's not grounded in some kind of airy-fairy state or some abstraction about who we are. The final responsibility is in every one of us and in what is right here—nowhere else. As long as we are seeking for something, we are trying to get out of the here-and-now in some way, but the here-and-now is really all we've got.

OUR TRUE IDENTITY

CHAPTER SIX

THE NATURE OF BEING HUMAN

There is much confusion about the nature of being human and about the nature of existence altogether. A basic understanding of what we are is directly related to a basic understanding of the nature of existence, because fundamentally we are inseparable from the nature of existence itself.

The nature of existence and the nature of being human are one and the same, and to not understand one is to not understand the other. We have only one way of knowing that we exist, and that is through open intelligence. In fact, without open intelligence we would have no knowledge of our existence. We've been trained to believe that our mind is what knows; however, the mind isn't really a *thing*. Instead, it is an abstraction and a descriptive framework that is only known due to awareness.

Lots of teachings say that everyone is already free, but then it will be maintained that the individual is imperfect and needs to be fixed. That is contradictory and quite unfortunate really, because there is no one to be fixed.

WHAT'S LOOKING?

When we look out through our eyes, what is it exactly that is looking? If one looks for what is looking, the conclusion is not quite as definitive as psychology textbooks might tell us. What's looking is always looking. It's impossible that it not be looking. When this looking is looked for, nothing is found. If we look within ourselves for what's looking, we can't really say where looking is located.

Our looking is in fact the looking of everything; it isn't the looking of an isolated individual. If we only know ourselves as an individual identity, then we might say, "Oh yes; my individual identity is located here in me. This is who I am. It is I who is looking out at the world." However, there is in fact no individual. Our identity is not fixed by the consolidation of factors of our personal history—our memory, people, places and things we've known or actions we've taken in life.

If we relax and let the looking be *as it is*, the whole idea about the looking being from within the skin line of an individual person dissolves. If we look for what's looking, we actually don't find anything specific or substantial. What we do find is purity, natural perfection and a vital emptiness that can't be located anywhere within our skin line. Looking out from all phenomena is the same looking. A name for this looking is open intelligence; it is open intelligence that is looking. We can never isolate an identity other than our identity as open intelligence.

We live in a world of images, but more importantly, we live as *the looking* that lives within every single one of those images. There isn't any looking separate from any image that appears; the looking is within the image, and the image occurs in, of, as, and through the looking. This is very important for us to understand.

REAL FREEDOM

We are trained from an early age that we are an individual identity and that this identity is fundamental to us. People give us various descriptions about ourselves, like for example, "You're a boy, your name is this or that and you're from this kind of family," and we believe this. One after another all these ideas are accumulated into a personality, and we cling to these ideas tenaciously because we don't know anything else. Our parents tell us lots of things and we also learn about ourselves from others, and we start to decide who we are by using these descriptions to form an identity.

But it's much easier to not have to appear to be anything! Freedom is the complete release from holding to any point of view, so that we no longer need to hold to any beliefs about who we are. If we are truly fortunate, our life circumstances will unfold in such a way that we will be forced to *not* see ourselves as a personal identity any longer. To not see ourselves as a person with a worthwhile reputation or a worthless reputation and to not see ourselves as negative or positive data—this is what gives us the freedom that is beyond all conventional limitations, and this is the only real freedom there is.

There's never any real freedom in what requires a descriptive support. Whether we see ourselves as good or bad or neutral, or whether others see us as good or bad or neutral, all of these are nothing other than data, and none of them are a worthwhile pursuit at all.

Even though we may think that the descriptions about our life constitute our identity, they never really do. We know that anything that we believe as constituting our identity can be snatched away, and this is why we have an underlying anxiety that things might not quite be right. We can't rely on the datum of our personal identity, just as we can't rely on any other datum.

Even if we do consolidate all kinds of factors that we consider to be necessary to our self-identity—money, power, prestige, people, places, things, food, the right sexual experiences—we never trust them completely and we are always looking for more. There is always the underlying anxiety, "It isn't quite right yet. I need something else to make it right."

Many of us have had a lifelong project of rehabilitating our ego in order to make it into a better ego. As a result, we have essentially spent our whole life in rehab, so to speak, and everyone else is pretty much in rehab as well! When everyone is pretty much in rehab, it's a scary situation.

Getting real with who we are doesn't mean figuring out our personality, our neuroses, our disorders or our personality type. All those are merely data, so that makes them easy to deal with. If we're worried about our ego, we need to remember that when it appears, it's only a datum appearing in open intelligence. That's it.

There isn't anything that has ever been solidified or made into anything. Anyone who tells us that we have an ego is way off course. By the power of short moments of open intelligence repeated many times, we loosen up the hold of this identity that we've established ourselves to be.

There never is a moment where all the right data congregate, other than in the split second release of the here-and-now. That is the perfect moment of the congregation of all data—the total, pure, lucid presence. The crystal clarity of what is spontaneously self-releasing can never be grasped, caught or measured. It is always immeasurable, always fleeting, always pure.

THE GREAT RELAXATION

Twenty-eight years ago I realized that I had placed great faith in being a "someone" who could control what was going on inside myself and who could gather together various intellectual, spiritual and psychological tools and get a handle on things. I aspired to organize and order my perfect world, and I wanted to keep all my thoughts, emotions, sensations and experiences at bay, but that never happened! The more I tried to organize my life and put it into some kind of order, the more disorganized and disorderly it became, and I could see that my efforts were leading nowhere.

I really wanted to be somebody in the world, and I was quite good at being somebody. Whatever I had thought that I might want, I had it. I had a wonderful husband, wonderful children, a wonderful career, plenty of money and I was able to buy anything I wanted and go anywhere I wanted to go—but it led absolutely nowhere.

Because I could see that it was leading nowhere, I felt hopeless and desperate. I thought, "What's going to happen here? Everything I've been told would work to make me a happy person hasn't made me happy. I don't feel mature, and I don't feel capable of living the rest of my life." I would look out for decades ahead of me, and it looked very bleak indeed.

I started to examine myself and the nature of my own experience. At the time I was having a lot of very disturbing thoughts and emotions related to some things that had happened in my life, and there wasn't any way I could stop these disturbing emotions and thoughts. They just kept coming in great tidal waves, one right after the other. Because it was hopeless to try and stop them from coming, at some point I reached a level of desperation where I finally thought, "I give up; I can't do anything about all this."

The amazing thing is that when I just relaxed, I experienced a totally great relief. When I experienced this great relief, it became clear to me that there was something about me that I hadn't been familiar with, and whatever it was, it was the basis of my entire existence. I saw that the idea that there was someone in control was a fiction. No matter how much I had thought that there was someone there, there wasn't anyone there!

Whether it was the thought of "someone there" or "no one there," great relief was present in the totality of the experience. This is a relief that is always naturally present, regardless of how we imagine ourselves to be. Neither the idea of "no one there" nor the idea of "someone there" is what we want. We don't want some kind of egoless, vacant state going on any more than we want the idea of someone going on. What we really want is to experience ourselves as we truly are, and we experience ourselves as we really are in open intelligence.

For me the disturbing states were predominant at first, but I could see that these states just appeared and disappeared in complete relief and relaxation. There wasn't anything I needed to do about them. The whole idea of feeling that I needed to do something about them had kept me all tangled up in knots, but I saw that they were self-freeing, self-releasing and spontaneously resolving in this sense of great relief that was at the basis of everything. Again and again as much as I could I would just return for short moments to this basis of everything.

With my total commitment to that, from the very beginning I very quickly started to attain confidence and clarity. It was a clarity that couldn't really be described—I just was smarter somehow! I was smarter in relation to myself, and I was smarter in relation to all situations I was in. I had a quiet but also piercing knowing that was at the basis of everything. I had been miserable because of these disturbing states, but now I was experiencing them as appearing within a great sense of relief and relaxation. That's what I mean by a quiet but piercing knowing. It is a very clear knowing, an absolute clarity about the nature of who we are.

As this became more obvious in me, it became so clear that everyone is exactly the same. This great relief, this great relaxation of short moments repeated many times is simple, clear and directly accessible for everyone. It is fundamental and basic to everyone's experience.

GLOBAL HUMAN COMMUNITY

It's important to understand that most of us have been educated by our family, our schools and our environment in a way that is quite off base, and we have actively chosen to adopt the information that was offered to us. We learn all sorts of things: for instance that our identity is based on a past, a present and a future and that the totality of all our viewpoints—past, present and future—constitutes our identity. We hear ideas about psychology and science and other things, and we accept these things as true. But our true identity can never be fully understood by descriptive frameworks.

Only when we understand that we have electively taken on this information can we also feel that we are empowered to change our relationship to it. If we say that someone else has educated us improperly and we blame institutions or people for that, then we are automatically placing ourselves in a disempowered position of helplessness. We're blaming the people and institutions that imposed the ideas on us that have made us do whatever we're doing; however, it is essential to not consider oneself a victim of other people's actions.

We have relied on educational, governmental, religious, medical and spiritual authority figures to tell us what is true about our identity. We simply accepted whatever we were being told by different authority figures. Instead of relying on these authorities, we need to clearly understand the nature of our identity based on *our own experience* of that identity. Whatever the developmental process has been like for us, we have a right to choose a different developmental process right now.

For the first time in human history, due to the Internet and advanced forms of telecommunications, there is a great wealth of information available that cannot be controlled by authority. The whole idea of relying on structures of authority is collapsing, and human society is beginning to recognize its own unified power. When we recognize our own unified power, then we can organize for change as a global human community based on open intelligence and not on conventional beliefs and structures of authority.

We all want to somehow appear to be unique and original, but the only true uniqueness is the uniqueness of the natural perfection of open intelligence. If we want to bring uniqueness and originality to our passions and interests in life, that can only come from being completely familiar with open intelligence. From that vantage, we can contribute incredible things that simply aren't possible from point of view.

When we allow the relief and ease of open intelligence, then we have tremendous energy and vitality. We're an easeful and effortless source of energy, love and clarity that never gets tied up in conventions of any kind. It leaves all convention behind, no matter how established the tradition may be.

There's a complete understanding of all the conventional descriptions and an ability to operate within them with great ease—without any need to rely on them exclusively. What is beyond all systems, all approaches, all methods and all practices becomes clear to us through gaining familiarity with our own open intelligence in a very direct and straightforward way.

Whatever our own data are, they are the basis for our realization of open intelligence. When we are no longer limited by our data, we become a source of immediate benefit to ourselves and to others. We no longer need to rely on other people making things okay for us, and we don't get caught up in making other people feel burdened because of what has happened to us in our lives.

There aren't any tricks or gimmicks, methods or practices that are needed—each one of us is given whatever we need. Free-flowing wisdom is naturally responsive in a very direct and loving way to every single person. By the words spoken and the energy present, each person feels responded to in a deeply personal way. When we know who we are, we have the capacity to love others unconditionally. That's really amazing, but that's what complete, totally open love is. There's never anything else that is required for living life.

RELYING ON THE BASIC STATE

It is so common for us to want to stand out in some way, and I have engaged in this sort of thing myself. When I was a young woman I relied on my supposed beauty, and I got a lot of attention through that, but at some point I realized that it was a dead end. Relying on beauty was never going to give me any kind of permanent well-being.

To try to make ourselves desirable or appealing to others is simply a way of deluding ourselves about who we really are. Why rely on all these ideas about being attractive? Instead, rely on the basic state. The basic state clears up all confusion and we have total objectivity, which is crystal clear discernment about everything that appears. We're no longer all wrapped up in the projects of the personal self, because we have found that our true identity is not the personal self, but the basic state.

So, when the next urge comes up to go off on some kind of self-identification project—simply relax. There is something that is so much better than getting all wrapped up in these ideas about attractiveness and popularity. It is in making the commitment where the commitment is worth making: in the instinctive recognition of the basic state, and in that everything is taken care of. You can count on this without fail.

If you're looking for your inner or outer beauty, for the perfect weight, for the perfect idea, emotion, sensation or experience to have, ground yourself in instinctive recognition of the basic state. Clear everything up all at once. Why trouble yourself with all the projects that are endless, countless and ceaseless? If you want to really find out who you are, rely on the basic state. Rely on that which is unaffected by birth, life and death. This is where you're going to find what you're looking for.

THE MANY TUNES OF "I"

We wake up in the morning and some days it may be a happy thought pattern, but other days it may be an unhappy thought pattern—it just depends on what tunes are playing that day. It's like having random compilations on an iPod, where we don't know what we're going to hear next. The iTunes play according to our particular version of "I"! Our particular tunes of "I" constantly appear as if in a random play list, and that play list may go on and on for as long as we live.

We each have our own particular tunes. For one person it might be, "I'm stupid; I can't do anything." For another it might be, "Shut up and listen to me; I know what I am talking about." Whatever these tunes may be, they all have exactly the same basis. Whether we think we are the dullest person on earth or the brightest, or whether we think we're the craziest or the sanest, or whether we think we're the richest or the poorest, it is all situated in the same source.

When we begin to realize that open intelligence is the source of all those thoughts, then all the tunes that are playing aren't so compelling. We don't start singing along with every tune that comes up. Instead, we are enjoying stable open intelligence and the clarity therein.

We don't have more than this moment. If we allow everything to be *as it is* in this moment, then everything is spacious and open, and we will know what to do when the next tune comes along. We don't have to spend this moment worrying about the next moment or plummeting into past moments to try to make sense of them. The only way we are going to make sense of our past tunes or our future tunes is in the restfulness of right now.

CHAPTER SEVEN

THE ULTIMATE FRIEND

If a trainer wants to train other people about relief from data, that trainer needs to have permanent relief at all times in their own lives. He or she has to have a balanced vantage every single moment, night and day, before there is the capacity for the wisdom speech that cuts through everything. In true wisdom speech is the power to train others about that relief and to help them go beyond their data.

There may be one person in a million for whom having a trainer isn't necessary, but for the rest of us, having a trainer is crucial. If we meet trainers who have resolved their own data, they can be of tremendous benefit to us, because they can see everything about us that we can't see ourselves. So, if we have the guts and the gall, we can make ourselves fully available to them and let them love us along!

A trainer such as this is really the personification of love. It may not be our contemporary views on what love is, but it is in fact what love is. A person who can show us how to love ourselves and others is the best friend we'll ever have. They'll always love us; so at some point we realize, "Wow, there is nothing I can do to make this person not love me!"

We learn many conventional things about relationships, and most of what we learn is based on finding out who is buying into our data and who isn't. In a scenario like that, the people who buy into our data are our friends, and the ones who don't buy into our data won't be people we want to spend time with.

However, a relationship with a trainer is not this sort of conventional relationship.

Trainers come in all forms, but a trainer is above all else an ultimate friend. A trainer is someone who already has the decisive experience of fully-evident open intelligence in their life. If you have a difficult datum come up, you can talk to the trainer, and if they see something in you that needs to be looked at, they will be able to gently and lovingly support you in coming to terms with it. The trainer will know all your secret data.

What is called "skillful means" is an aspect of wisdom which manifests as expert guidance and assistance, and different trainers have different skillful means. Some trainers are very harsh, and so they might come at you with a fireball. Another approach is to shame, demean or degrade a person, which some trainers do, but there is one approach that works incredibly well: love. Love is the trainer's primary skillful means. Love overcomes all.

In my own experience of visiting teachers all over the world, I know there are many different styles of teaching, and this is what I have found conclusively: love always works, and love always has the most fruitful results.

PROFOUNDLY WISE

When we find within ourselves the love, compassion and clarity that are at the basis of every single thought, then we become profoundly wise—not just conventionally wise—and we are able to be of great benefit to ourselves and others. Anyone who has complete mental and emotional stability is first of all profoundly beneficial to themselves, and in whatever contacts that person has with other people, he or she will be profoundly beneficial to them without even having to try to do so. A person with complete mental and emotional stability can walk into a room and without saying anything have a beneficial impact on the situation.

It is profound, because this complete mental and emotional stability is the basis of human nature and the birthright of every single human being. Instinctively and intuitively we know that this is possible for us, even though we may not have known how to bring it about. When we are in the proximity of a person who has complete emotional and mental stability, that part of us that recognizes the stability responds to the presence of that in the other person. They don't have to say anything to us; their communication is beyond words. It doesn't have anything to do with blabbing about something or writing it down. It is just clear, and it soaks in whether someone wants it to or not. It is beyond wanting or not wanting.

ATTRACTION RATHER THAN PROMOTION

One of the questions that is asked very frequently is, "How can I get my friends and family interested in relying on short moments, many times?" I never encourage people to evangelize or promote the practice of short moments. The people close to us will be naturally attracted if they see changes in us because of our practice of short moments. That might then be an opening for them to become interested, but there is no need to try to get people involved who aren't interested. There will be plenty of people who will show up who *are* interested.

The question still comes up as to what we should do with people in our lives, such as our parents, partners and friends, who have no interest in short moments. The answer is that we can maintain our own practice of relying on short moments and follow the intelligent compassion that knows how to deal with everything in every single moment. Then we can go about life in a relaxed and carefree way and act skillfully when action needs to be taken and do what would be most beneficial for the people around us.

If we decide that it is our personal project to get everyone who deeply believes in their data to not believe in them, well, that is one way of going about life. Another way to go about life is to be interested in supporting the people who don't want to believe in their data any longer. There are lots of people who are ready to stop believing their data, and so it is best to wait for those people to show up.

People are either ready to hear about short moments or they aren't, and the ones who are ready will show up when it's right for them. It's always possible to engage in dialogues and debates with people, or one could simply stay with what one knows to be true and see who would be attracted to that. There isn't any need to try to convince someone who isn't interested.

We naturally want to reach out to people who are totally lost in their data, because we know what it feels like to be lost in stories and negative thinking. However, the training of short moments is not for those who need it; it is for those who want it. As people see changes in others, they will be attracted to try it out for themselves. The ones who want it can benefit from it, and more and more people will come along who do want it.

THE INTIMACY OF TRUE RELATING

It's absolutely extraordinary to see how people can live and work together from a perspective of clarity. Every one of our fondest dreams of how it might be to live and work with other people is realized with people who are gaining confidence in open intelligence. It's really astounding. Certainly everything that I ever dreamed could be possible in terms of human relationship is coming about, because people are able to come together so wonderfully from the perspective of open intelligence.

n we gain certainty in open intelligence, we come into
ct with other people who are doing the same, and as a
res. it we come together with a community of people who can
genuinely love us. They love us as we are, and they don't need
for us to be any particular way. They love us as all of our data
are appearing and as all of their own data are appearing. They
are not put off by anything that's happening, and they know
how to skillfully support us with whatever is happening for us.
We are together with people who love us without their needing
to have a reason to love us. What could be better than that?

All of life should be filled with the intimacy of true relating
that open intelligence allows. Even if for many years you have
settled for a limited vision of what is possible, you can start
right now by not settling for the same old thing. Maintain
confidence in open intelligence and you'll have all the strength
you need to see through any murky situations or relationships
you might currently be in.

You have to prove to yourself in your own experience that
open intelligence has power over everything. If you have
something that is really important to you which you want to
bring into being, then through the recognition of inherent open
intelligence, it can come about in a really marvelous and
effortless way. All the right people will come together to make
that possible and you'll find yourself surrounded by people who
are easygoing and powerful. So, you won't have to do things the
hard way anymore!

People are attracted by openness and a welcoming and
unbiased attitude. It is not what they hear that is necessarily
convincing for them; it's through seeing that the people who are
practicing short moments really are examples of what the
training describes. The great friendliness and warmth that are
present are so attractive and compelling, and people feel that
very intimately. They are attracted to it because it's what they
have always wanted for themselves.

When you gain certainty in open intelligence, you have much greater freedom in all aspects of your life. You are able to be anywhere and with anyone and still be okay. It doesn't mean you'll like the situation you are in all the time, but in yourself you'll be okay. To have this ability is urgently important for everyone in the world.

LIVING WITH PEOPLE IN A NATURAL WAY

If you're fully alert and awake, then when you're living with other people, in a natural way you can see what needs to be done. For example, if someone needs help doing a job, you could jump in and help in a very easeful and natural way. If there are household chores that need to be taken care of, you might quietly come forward and do the work without anyone else knowing about it. When people are alert to the needs of others there is an easy and open flow where everyone participates harmoniously together without any big to-do about who does what.

Once you realize this natural way of being in your own life, then you can share that with others. A part of realizing it within yourself is to share it with others. What else would anyone want to do? Even though you might be involved in a lot of other activities that are very important, you'll see how important it is for human society to be enriched more and more by this natural way of being together.

There are communities around the world where there are many people who are discovering their true nature, and they have the evidence of the love, service and collaborative work relationships that are clearly evident in open intelligence. When new people come, they are received and welcomed into the group. There is a genuine warm-heartedness; there is no gossip, backbiting or politics going on.

No one in a community such as that will ever tell you that you are a bad person or tell you to go away. It is a lifelong community. Even if a person wants to leave the community, the attitude would be, "Oh, we will miss you; come back any time." There are no subtle undertones of, "Do it our way or you are out of here."

Things can function very easily when individuals take leadership of themselves. By opening up to the true connection that is really possible among people, it becomes possible to participate together in a harmonious way. There is simply a flow where things get done without any sort of planning or assigning, and there is a real sweetness and warmth about it. All these are things that one sees with people living together in community who are at ease with their data.

THE TRAINING AND THE COMMUNITY

If you are interested in gaining certainty in open intelligence, it is helpful to surround yourself with people who are doing the same. This is the easy way to go. There are plenty of other people around the world with whom you can share community in this way, and to form community with other people who are free of hatred, arrogance, envy and fear is a very powerful way to live.

Being with a group of people in which everybody gets along is very special; everyone works for the mutual success of everyone else, and the expression is not just theoretical but is deeply rooted in everyone's daily experience. Imagine if all of human society were like that! By gaining certainty in open intelligence, even if you happen to be physically alone, you are never alone. You are in the community of the completely unchanging basic state that is unfailing and which will never let

1.

Take advantage of trainings that will resolve your
by hearing or reading trainings such as those, there
profound sense of peace and of knowing that everything is all
right. This profound sense of peace and knowing will grow in
you, and it will shine in you like light that emanates from the
sun.

Don't be sidetracked by trainings that aren't about the direct
experience of perfect open intelligence. Dedicate your whole
precious life to open intelligence, and make that primary above
all else. Soon you won't need to have a name for this direct
experience—you'll absolutely know in every single moment
what the nature of reality is. You'll experience complete and
total relief deeply within yourself in an unshakable and
indestructible way.

Other things in life are fleeting and impermanent; they are
spontaneous appearances in open intelligence that never last.
Place all of your effort in what is truly lasting. This is the course
of action you want to take for your life. Distraction by all kinds
of other things, as important as they may seem to be, will never
lead anywhere. Are all these activities going to give you
complete relief? Are they going to be there for you when you
are on your deathbed?

This is what you want to gain certainty in; everything else
will eventually be destroyed. If you live a life wrapped in
ordinary activities and keeping those as primary in your life, it's
like living your life with your head in the mouth of a crocodile.
Being wrapped up in ordinary activities can't sustain you over
the short term and it can't sustain you over the long term either.

You want to gain certainty in that which can never be
destroyed. Even if you are young, healthy, robust and have all
the things you want, all that will be taken away from you. At
some point you won't be young, healthy and robust, and you

won't be able to accumulate things or find them to be a source of satisfaction.

If you are young and healthy, begin gaining certainty in open intelligence right now. If on the other hand you are older and you have only now heard about the training of short moments, gain certainty in that right now. It is that which will always comfort you and bring you relief, no matter what. Know that the short moment of open intelligence that you are repeating many times will always be your mainstay and support.

INDWELLING CONFIDENCE

It is really a wonderful gift to have enthusiasm for discovering the true nature of being. Many of us have been enthusiastic about all kinds of things in our life: we see something new, we have great enthusiasm for it and we hope that it is going to solve our problems and make life better. For example, we might get a new self-help book, and while we are reading it we think, "I feel so great reading this book. This will solve my problem." Then we finish the book, and we might feel really good for a couple of days, but then before long, the enthusiasm wanes and we are looking for another book.

To discover the true nature of our being doesn't require any books or any looking. What we really want is not another book but the full introduction to our fundamental nature. When we have been introduced to our true nature and we come to know what that is, we can make a commitment to it. Yet, if we only make a partial commitment, then some of the time we will be relying on open intelligence, but the remainder of the time we will be applying antidotes to all of our data. If we make a one hundred percent commitment, then indwelling confidence develops, and with that confidence certainty comes about.

If commitment wanes and we decide that we are going to elaborate on our data and make a story out of them, or we decide to take on some methods or practices to try to make things better, that's a far cry from maintaining the full commitment to relying on open intelligence. Sometimes the commitment wanes, and that is just how it is, and this is something that occurs for many people. If our commitment wanes, then we need to turn to people who can wholeheartedly support us.

We are always committed to something—we are committed either to all of our data or to relying on open intelligence. We have the choice as to which commitment we will make.

THE FOUR MAINSTAYS

The Four Mainstays of Balanced View are meant to provide a continual resource of soothing energy, support and comfort to those who need it. One mainstay is the practice of short moments of open intelligence repeated many times until it becomes automatic; another is the trainer, a third is the training—the written trainings, the downloads, the books, the open intelligence calls—and then fourth, the worldwide community.

Contact with a trainer is very important. In the Western countries we're very accustomed to doing things on our own and being the sole manager of our life. If we are that way, it is possible that we will be uninterested in receiving help from people who could potentially contribute to us. If we remain fixed in this idea of being totally self-sufficient, not only will we not be able to see that people can support us, we might be especially resistant to the very people who could really contribute to us.

Resistance to asking for support is a point of view that really must be seen through, because it is very difficult for most people to resolve all of their data without support from people who have already resolved their own.

We have all kinds of data that we don't even think about. There are personal data that relate to our own particular life and how we've lived that life, and then there are also collective data. Included within that are gender and cultural data, and we may be completely blind to many of them. Someone who has resolved all their data can be tremendously supportive in clarifying these different issues and helping us to look at what is going on with us. The people to rely on for help are those who have had significant experience with relying on open intelligence and who have mastered the challenges of ordinary life like money, sex, work, depression, food issues and relationships. The data in their lives have been outshone by open intelligence, just like the the light of the planets and stars at night is outshone by the daytime sun.

If we want to understand how to have a good relationship, for example, we don't want to go to someone who has dysfunctional relationships and ask them how to have a good relationship! To learn about skillful relating, we want to go to someone who demonstrates that in their own life. In a similar way, we wouldn't want to go to someone for advice on money issues who hasn't learned how to handle their money in a skillful way.

When we are having a challenge in maintaining open intelligence with any of these important issues, we can rely on one of the Four Mainstays. If we find that we cannot maintain open intelligence and we're going off into all kinds of stories about all our data, then we really need to reach out for support *immediately*. Why prolong the agony?

When we are challenged by data and all wrapped up in the story about them and adding more and more stories on top of the original story—that's definitely the time to contact our trainer. Many times when we're lost in a big story, another person can just say one sentence, and we are able to recognize open intelligence immediately. Whenever challenging things occur in our lives, the trainer is invaluable, the community is invaluable, the training is invaluable and relying on open intelligence is invaluable.

Section Three
Open Intelligence Expressed in Our Day-to-Day Lives

REAL LIFE CIRCUMSTANCES, REAL LIFE RESPONSES

CHAPTER EIGHT

BEING IN CONNECTION WITH EVERYONE

If you feel out of connection with someone or you are afraid to talk to them or you feel alienated by them, well, what a great opportunity to be at ease with your data! If you are afraid someone is going to scream and yell at you, how is the fear of the actual screaming or yelling itself going to affect open intelligence? It doesn't affect your open intelligence and it doesn't affect theirs either. So, what is there to be afraid of?

If you have been afraid of people who are angry, then to remain relaxed and easeful while the anger flows all around you is going to be a very, very powerful introduction to open intelligence. When I was growing up, I developed a fear of angry people. I didn't react against them with anger, but I had a lot of other clever strategies of manipulating situations to either quell their anger or rearrange the circumstance so the angry people wouldn't take over.

Once I gained certainty in open intelligence, I found that there was no reason to be afraid of angry people. I saw that no one's anger could ever affect open intelligence. I found myself in a few situations with people who were going off either at me or someone else, but nothing happened.

Any of these opportunities you have for a short moment of open intelligence are very valuable—and exceedingly powerful. You see that you can be in all situations without impediment. It wouldn't have to only be with people who are angry; it could also be with frightening circumstances that arise—a feeling or emotion that scares you, a feeling of being inferior to other people or being nervous, uneasy, angry, sad or depressed or whatever the particular point of view is. But none of those need affect you.

Everybody else could be upset, distracted and disoriented, but through the instinctive recognition of the basic state, you can be with everything in a relaxed way. Short moments, many times in these situations is exceedingly powerful. You begin to really stand tall, unruffled by all circumstances and able to skillfully respond from a balanced view.

COMPLETELY RESOLVING FEAR

One of the great fears that we have is being thought of as being stupid, and we will do anything to avoid that fear. Let's say that somebody says to us, "You're an idiot!" then we may feel all forlorn and worthless, and we might not know what to do with those feelings. But wide awake within all the emotions involved with being told that we are stupid is the here-and-now of total perfection.

By not believing in the story that surrounds these thoughts, we completely transform our "stupidity" into a moment of brilliant clarity. With certainty in open intelligence, we see through all these things that have always pushed our buttons. When we do get our buttons pushed and our habitual thoughts and emotions get started up, it's in that moment that instinctive recognition of open intelligence is crucial. This is the way to completely resolve the fear that comes from any of these experiences.

It might seem odd to use the example of stupidity, but how many of us have ever felt stupid? These very painful data come up for all of us; yet, we may feel that we're the only one who has them, and these types of feelings can be extremely isolating.

Maybe one of our extreme ideas is, "I can't
anything; I'm really pretty worthless." But when t/
where does it appear? Wide-awake within the feeli ⌣
worthless is the here-and-now of total perfection. Everyone and
everything rests in the here-and-now of natural perfection. No
matter what the ideas may be, no matter what label is applied to
them, they all appear in natural perfection.

AT EASE WITH ANYTHING AT ALL

Someone might have a talk with me, and they might tell me
about something terrible they're going through, like for instance
their husband or wife leaving them. I can feel what they're
saying very deeply, and I empathize with their pain, but along
with that I often tell them, "Your wife or husband has left you to
be with someone else—what a wonderful opportunity for you.
Congratulations!"

If something like that did happen to you—your partner left
you, you had a heart attack or you lost all your money in a
financial collapse—all kinds of circumstantial thoughts, 9-18-12
emotions and sensations associated with that incident would
follow. However, what would fundamentally change throughout
the entire course of events? Nothing. What remains steadfast 2
and complete is the here-and-now, nakedly seeing from within. l (ke
It's always like that, and it can never be any other way. ⟵ this,

Let's say that something did happen as difficult as your
husband or wife leaving you. You could be writhing in pain, or
you could be calm as can be—or somewhere in between—but
even as you have all the variety of possible experiences, nothing
actually changes. This is the nature of the here-and-now—
unchanging, indestructible, just *as it is.* No matter what appears
within it, it is unflappable, unflinching, unmoving. It allows for
everything equally.

What does that say about us? It says that when we relax our hold on trying to make things be a certain way, then we begin to experience everything *as it is*, and we experience ourselves exactly as we are. There may have been all kinds of thoughts, emotions and sensations we've been avoiding, but once we give up the avoidance and we are as we are—open-minded and openhearted—then we can be at ease with anything at all that appears.

Let go the grip!, 9-18-12

YOUR OWN CLEAR EXAMPLE

If someone wants to argue with you and starts provoking you, that doesn't mean that you have to be in conflict with them. You can stand firm without allowing yourself to go into any of the difficulties that are often present in a situation like that. From wide-open clarity you have a lot more options about how to deal with people who are criticizing or provoking you. By securing yourself in clarity and allowing everything to be *as it is*, with no need to act impulsively or compulsively, you become clearer and clearer about what is going to lead to the best solution in that situation. You'll see what measures you need to take from clarity.

You won't see the solution if you're lost in the conflict and all tangled up in the outpouring of emotions. By relying on open intelligence rather than the data that come up in a challenging situation, you can have a good and peaceful life, even in the midst of very trying circumstances. With more and more people committing to that, there can be more and more people who have an easeful and peaceful life.

It doesn't matter what anyone else is up to—be your own best ally. You don't want to allow someone else's negative data to rule you. With people who have exceedingly negative data, it may not be possible to get them to change. They need to come to the point themselves where they actually want to change.

There may be many ways in which that change can come about, but one of the ways that the change is made possible is through your own clear example.

As much as you might like everyone else to see the light or to undergo some kind of radical change, the best way to affect the lives of others is by focusing on yourself in this way. Keep the focus right there. This doesn't mean that you are self-obsessed or inattentive to the needs of others; it means that you are alert to your own data and you are not getting lost in your or other people's stories.

It can really be painful to see what other people are doing to themselves, but it is not your job to make their decisions for them. You have to decide which mountain you want to climb. If you scramble around trying to climb a lot of different mountains, then you'll never master one.

Don't allow yourself to be yanked off on somebody else's trip. If you've been wrapped up with people who are completely involved in negative disregard of themselves and others, now you can simply and easily inch away from that. You don't have to keep hanging out with the same people who are so extremely lost in their negative data. By strengthening yourself in open intelligence you'll see that this is the case. Even if you momentarily fail to remember open intelligence and you get into some kind of negative conversation or circumstance with another person, as you recognize that you have done so, you can immediately return to open intelligence through a short moment of instinctive recognition.

You'll see that you can have a life that you never dreamt possible. If you wrap yourself up in all kinds of conventional ways of dealing with life, it may seem impossible to be free of wholly negative circumstances, but as you gain certainty in open intelligence, you see you're totally free; you've never needed to be wrapped up in situations that diminish you. The very least you can do is to give yourself this incredible gift.

I could sit here and talk about this until I'm blue in the face, but there isn't any way that your freedom is going to be recognized without your cooperation. It is recognized through the continual willingness to see who you are in a very fundamental sense and to never step away from that for any reason.

You want to give yourself everything you possibly can in this life; you really do, and you're the only one who can do that. This is where the rubber meets the road—it's in standing firm and holding to your own true nature.

COMPLETE EASE WITH THE FEAR OF ABANDONMENT

In a short moment of open intelligence, there is no description to worry about; there are no mental gymnastics about everything that went on in the past, what is going on now or what will be going on in the future. Even if there is some kind of spontaneous thought that occurs about a past or a future, it is no longer something that causes distress.

For instance, maybe we're in an intimate relationship, and the thought might arise, "Oh, I'm so afraid that my partner is going to leave me," and the next thought comes, "I was abandoned when I was a little kid, and I've been abandoned throughout my life, so that's why I will be abandoned by this partner," then yet another thought comes, "I'm the kind of person that people abandon," and so on. By following on with the innumerable thoughts that proceed from the initial thought, we create a story about ourselves.

We think, "I am a person with a story, and whatever my story is, that's who I am. If I want to get over my fear of abandonment, then I'm going to have to create a new and better story that involves not being abandoned." So, we may go out and look for another partner to give us a new story about not being abandoned, and when we find that new person who we're sure won't abandon us, we feel that we can now enjoy a relationship without having any fear of abandonment.

However, the only way to truly enjoy a relationship is to be at complete ease with the fear of abandonment and all other fears. Fear of abandonment is a thought that occurs to everyone who has ever had a relationship of any kind. In all honesty, *everyone* will be abandoned in every relationship, because either we'll die or the people we are attached to will die. It may seem like the fear of abandonment is just a form of paranoia, but in fact it's entirely true!

If we believe in the fear of abandonment, then it's going to be real to us, and we'll have to have a story about it. On the other hand, we can examine its nature when it appears: "Where is it really located? Can I say that it is something? Does it have a color or shape? Is there someone here experiencing the fear of abandonment?" By relying on open intelligence we come to see that the story we have had about the fear of abandonment isn't as fixed as it had seemed to be.

We might have said before, "I have the fear of abandonment, and I have it all day and I've had it all my life." But we can come to see that in fact these sorts of thoughts and emotions come and go in flash instants. The thoughts appear, stay for a while, recede and then reappear. We might not think about abandonment until later when we wrongly conclude, "That feeling of abandonment has been with me for every moment of the day." We actually don't have an unending stream of sequential thoughts on the same subject—it just seems that we do.

Our primary identity is always open intelligence, and every single one of our thoughts is an appearance of open intelligence.

By understanding our true identity as open intelligence, we are a lot more relaxed with the other information about ourselves.

To recognize the basic state of open intelligence is the truest story. There's no getting out of open intelligence. No matter what kind of story comes up, it is never going to be in any place other than in open intelligence. By recognizing this in each moment of experience, the whole of life is much more easeful and relaxed.

THE CONTEXT FOR DECISION-MAKING

When we are all wrapped up in our data, often we just don't know what to do. We don't know how to choose the right relationship, we don't know where we should live, we don't know how to be fully satisfied with our work, and one of our big things is that we really have a tough time making decisions. When we are lost in all of these data, it is like being in a dense forest, and we are so confused that we are willing to look anywhere for hope.

When we are lost in the dense forest and have to make decisions, we look up and see all the trees and we think, "Well, I am going to choose this tree and that tree and the other tree in the forest, and that is going to be my decision." Then the decision is made, but we are still lost in the dense forest, and we are wondering whether we made the right decision or not. We continue to wander in the forest of point of view, and this is what our life feels like when we are obsessed with all the doubts involved in making the decision.

When we begin to rely on short moments many times, rather than being so identified with all the trees in the dense forest, we are noticing more the basis of everything. We start to see that we really don't have to worry. Getting all wrapped up in worrying and negative thinking is a choice—it really is—so we see the trade-off.

By recognizing inherent open intelligence rather than spinning off into habitual decision-making methods, we find that there's an ease that's always the case. It is in that inherent ease that we find the most profound solution to the situation we are trying to decide about. It's not in spinning out the story about everything that's going on. For any situation that requires a decision, the best decision is going to come from this naked ease and clarity of open intelligence.

SKILL IN DAILY LIFE

"Good conduct" is generally defined as corralling our data into some notion of goodness. We act in a certain way, we think in a certain way, we speak in a certain way and that is called good conduct. When we engage in "good conduct" we may feel good about ourselves and we feel that we are contributing to the world; however, to think of ourselves only in that limited way is very de-energizing. We are not able to really experience the tremendous energy that is available in open intelligence, and we are not able to realize our full potential as human beings.

That energy comes about by releasing ourselves from the need to see data as good, bad or neutral. This is a very key point. This energy that is noticed from the first short moment of the instinctive recognition of open intelligence includes mental and emotional stability, insight, compassion and skill in daily activities. It is a very powerful energy that cannot be accessed by trying to shape our conduct in some sort of contrived way based on positive, negative or neutral data.

The skillful knowing of how to act in the most powerful, supremely creative way comes from the instinctive recognition of open intelligence. It doesn't come from looking at all the data and trying to decide how to shuffle them around into the right picture of what we should be and do.

rity, that clear open sky of awareness, is filled with of wisdom. Open intelligence isn't something to get ?ady present. No matter what you're involved in, if you want to open up a greater space of creativity or to be able to resolve a challenging conflict, go to open intelligence—do not go to data.

More and more all the words you speak and the actions you take are the words and actions of that powerful reality of wisdom. There's nothing more creative than that reality. It sees in a way in which data simply cannot see. Data cannot capture the super-complete open space of the creative impulse of the universe. *cool sentence, 9-20-12*

Your supremely creative and completely powerful self is in that moment of open intelligence. As you get more acquainted with open intelligence, you'll be filled with a true power that doesn't come from descriptions. It comes from the vast openness of the nature of reality that is always and forever wise and good.

NO MORE DRAMA

Many of us have trained ourselves to live from one drama to the next. Especially in the self-help culture people love to share their dramas. When we learn to relate to ourselves and to others in a problem-oriented way, it's because we see ourselves as a problem and we see other people as a problem. If we think that there is something wrong with us that needs to be fixed, then we are going to think that there's something wrong with other people and that they also need to be fixed.

Sometimes we can be together with another person for decades listening to their dramas as they listen to ours, and we have a sort of cooperation where we acknowledge each other's stories. "I'll listen to you if you'll listen to me, and we'll be co-hostages in drama and trauma." Some of us think we've got it

96

made when we have people who will co-sign our stories in this way, but if we are living a life of drama and trauma, then we are only living a story-based existence.

We may eventually want to seek relief in one way or another from the disturbing emotions brought on by our dramas. We seek this relief by avoiding the disturbing emotions, replacing them with something else or indulging them in various ways. We might take the edge off with booze or other drugs, with sex, food, money or shopping sprees, but whatever the antidote may be, it will never really provide total relief.

These are just temporary antidotes that look like they are going to provide relief, but they never really do. To reach for the same antidotes over and over again expecting different results is a form of insanity. So we really need to ask ourselves: why keep doing something over and over again that provides no lasting relief?

What are the options other than reaching for antidotes? Well, there is an option for all of humankind to rely on, and that is to recognize inherent open intelligence for short moments, many times until it becomes spontaneous. This is a solution that is fostered by realizing that our basic nature is already one of goodness and not one of dramas and traumas. When we recognize inherent open intelligence and we get to know the fundamental condition of our existence, then we no longer relate to people through a story-based existence of dramas and traumas.

OUR INNATE POTENTIAL

There are a lot of popular self-improvement programs around these days, but the thing about self-improvement programs is that they so easily fall apart. For instance, we may have tried to create a certain type of life through positive affirmations, such as, "I am intelligent and capable; I am happy; I am rich and famous." It could be that these things are all happening for us, but most likely they aren't! The strategy falls apart very quickly, and then we're back where we started. To try to get all these things into our lives is really not the best way to utilize our time and energy.

When it comes to understanding the purpose of human life and our own innate potential, we have to ask ourselves, "What is my ultimate power in terms of living a happy life in this moment? Have any of these self-improvement programs or positive affirmations ever brought me the peace and satisfaction I have sought?" The beauty of relying on open intelligence is that there is increasing soothing energy, an increasing feeling of well-being as well as an increasing confidence in open intelligence—something which these self-improvement programs cannot provide on a lasting basis.

What is called for is familiarity with the nature of existence. We could call this the super-intelligence that is at the basis of everything and which has power over everything. It rules over all descriptive frameworks: those of money, position, possessions, self-esteem, success and anything else one could strive for through self-improvement programs. By gaining confidence and certainty in this super-intelligence, a whole world opens up to us that we never knew existed.

FEARLESS IN THE FACE OF FEAR

When strong fear arises in us, our tendency may be to seek out something that's going to stop our fear. We might look for the right book that will show us how to never be afraid again, we might take a medication that will deal with the fear or we might try to live in such a way that we can avoid fearful situations.

But there is another choice: we can maintain open intelligence for short moments, many times, and as we do so we come to experience the fearlessness of open intelligence, which *inseparability of open intelligence + "Data"*

is being fearless in the face of fear. When fear appears, open intelligence is the fearless basis of that fear. This is what nonduality means: the not two-ness of everything.

When we are afraid of our own thoughts and emotions, we can feel very uncomfortable within ourselves. We can't stop these thoughts and emotions from coming, and we never know what form they will take. So, if we are looking to get rid of fear, then we'll always be disappointed. This is why it is of crucial importance to gain certainty in open intelligence.

We can't stop fears, and we don't want to delude ourselves into thinking that we can. We can't count on circumstances or other people to make everything safe and all right, but we can count on ourselves. If something really, really terrifying should happen in which our lives might even be threatened, if we have fully gained certainty in open intelligence, then even though there may be a lot of fear coming up during the terrifying event, our connection will be with calm, peaceful open intelligence rather than with all the fear.

Everything that appears is filled with fearless open intelligence. Even if fear appears in a totally gut-wrenching form, its nature is fearless open intelligence and nothing else. This is what is recognized in a short moment of the instinctive recognition of the inseparability of open intelligence and data.

COMPLETELY COUNT-ON-ABLE

Whether you're looking for the health of your thinking, health of your emotions or health of your body, that health is in short moments of open intelligence. So, if you do things like yoga, jogging, walking or whatever it might be, these are things to do for fun and enjoyment, but they won't lead to pure and perfect open intelligence. If you're walking, running, swimming, doing yoga or ballet or whatever you might enjoy—and you are abiding in short moments during that time—then you'll not only enjoy whatever you're doing more, but you will also be grounding yourself in your ultimate nature. *pear intelligence*

Westerners especially are very result-driven people; we want results from everything we do. If we put a comb to our hair, we want beautiful hair to be the result. When we're doing yoga in our ordinary flabby body, we have a picture in our mind of the body we want to have. This is what I mean by result-driven.

The only way to break through all this is in short moments. All the perfection we're looking for is in that short moment. That is where complete clarity is, complete power, complete emotional and mental stability, complete compassion, complete skillfulness—it's all in that short moment. Not only that, it's easy to take short moments many times. The momentum of that quickly picks up speed for everyone who relies on it. Why does it quickly pick up speed? Because one comes to see that it is reliable and trustworthy. In that first short moment, there is complete relief and a complete power of wisdom, and so it is count-on-able. We can really count on it, whereas we can't count on data to bring us relief.

The perfection that we're always driving ourselves towards is in that short moment, but it's not going to be a kind of perfection that we have imagined or dreamt of, because it is beyond imagination. Let's just say that it's amazing!

TOTAL RELIEF

Many of us have spent years working very hard in order to accomplish a lot. We effort and achieve and effort and achieve some more until we say, "What am I going to do now after all this effort and achievement?" The ideas we have that at some point we would attain satisfaction and fulfillment are never really realized. The recognition of this can be a very dismal experience, but it is also wonderful, because seeing that there is nothing to be achieved is really a crucial recognition.

All kinds of things c
confusion, desperation,
that seem so upsetting,
the same underlying b₂
of these appearances, ₐ
experience the great re
It then becomes natu
effortless way, just a
out of it.

The basic state is
leads to total relief,
compassion. The more relief we expeᵢᵥᵢ
open and compassionate we feel. These things that we have
always wanted—to love and be loved, to belong, to be free—are
realized in the complete ease of our own being.

There is nowhere else to look. If we are looking anywhere
else, it will never be found. If we are looking anywhere else we
are always at least one step away, or maybe many steps away.
When we already are who we are, how could recognizing who
we are be a difficult task?

CHAPTER NINE

___

G IN ALL SITUATIONS WITHOUT IMPEDIMENT

no doubt that all kinds of terrible things can happen to life. There are things that occur that are very unexpected, d we never know when they will occur. We can't even predict what will happen in the next minute, let alone what is going to happen during the rest of our lives.

It is important to know what our mainstay is throughout all those circumstances. When we gain confidence in the innately stable nature of our own being, then we know that we can be in all situations without impediment. We know that we can have the naturally occurring indwelling confidence of the stability of our own nature to rely on. This is very important.

We don't have to be in any special circumstance. We can be at work or school or having fun with our friends, and whatever situation we're in, it's a perfect opportunity to rely on open intelligence.

THE BIRTH OF TRUE COMPASSION

Let's say you've felt great contentment in your life, but then all of a sudden one of your parents dies unexpectedly or your child dies or you find out that you have a terrible illness. If the contentment you were experiencing was only based on inner psychological states or outer circumstances, it will almost surely disappear in the face of such an overwhelming event.

If you haven't learned that every appearance—including grief, illness and loss of loved ones—is always resting in the fundamental condition of the naturally settled state, then when these difficult events occur, you won't know what to do. You will be totally filled with stories about why these kinds of things could happen and what you need to do about them.

Perhaps in the beginning it might *seem* to be completely impossible to rely on open intelligence with extremely afflictive states, but that doesn't mean that it *is* impossible. I can speak from my own experience. I had been in a very traumatic situation and everything had been totally turned upside down; yet, I found that it was possible for me to be at ease as extremely afflictive states like terror, bewilderment, confusion and paranoia arose. I came to see that anyone can be at ease even when afflictive states arise.

It is only in recognizing open intelligence that we can understand the non-threatening nature of afflictive states. By repeatedly recognizing open intelligence for short moments many times, we strengthen ourselves, so that when afflictive states appear, we can recognize open intelligence from within them. We recognize open intelligence to be inseparable from whatever is appearing, like the color blue is inseparable from the sky. When we are able to do so, that really provides the greatest benefit.

When afflictive states come up—rely on open intelligence! Don't analyze, refine, describe or attempt to figure out what's appearing in any way. Go right to open intelligence, nowhere else. As we rely more and more on open intelligence, we begin to see the lack of separation between happiness and suffering. What that means in a practical way is that, whether we are having an easy time or we are experiencing very challenging circumstances, we are totally at ease and serene.

We are profoundly aware that, whatever our own joys or sufferings might be, the same joys and suffering happen for all beings—and not just for us. We stop relating to ourselves in terms of "poor me" and start seeing more clearly that joys and suffering are experiences common to every human being. This is the birth of true compassion.

FEELING GOOD AT ANY STAGE OF LIFE

For many of us the story of our adult life might read like this: "Oh, maybe if I can find someone who loves me, things will get better." Then once we get married or have a partner, we see, well, that's not going to do it, so then we think that having a baby together will be the key. We have the baby, but the baby doesn't give us what we are seeking either. Now we have the partner and the baby, and not only do we have our own thoughts, emotions, sensations and experiences, but now we're responsible for these other people and their data, too.

Then we think, "Okay, the right job, that's going to do it. When I get into this right job, it will give me a chance to spread my wings and have more fulfillment." Then we get into the job and that doesn't do it. We get the house, the car, the clothes, the food and the entertainment, but then we realize, "Well, none of this really did it. It must be retirement; that's the thing that will give it to me. I won't have this dull job anymore, and I will have accumulated all the things I need. Then I'm really going to feel good."

The retirement age rolls around and we are able to retire, but we find that this didn't work either. Now the bones are starting to ache and the body is falling apart, and not only that, there is no way to fix it. No jogging, bungee jumping, mountain climbing or self-help programs will make us physically robust again. We can't do the things that we did when we were younger, and we are just left as we are. It is the rare elder who is able to have a positive attitude throughout the aging process.

If we are lucky enough to rely on short moments, repeated many times, we have the opportunity to write a totally different story. We acquire the coping mechanisms to deal with what comes up at any stage of life, particularly later in life.

PERMANENT PEACE OF MIND

Feelings of inadequacy, disappointment and failure may come up for us, but it is important to ask ourselves what these things are ultimately. What, for instance, is failure? The ultimate failure is to not recognize and gain confidence in one's own true nature.

There can be no bigger disappointment than being controlled by conventional ideas about who we are. There is nothing to be found in fulfilling our ideas about ourselves or other people's ideas about us. Rather than going for all these dead-end ideas, we have the perfect opportunity to gain certainty in open intelligence when these thoughts of inadequacy or failure arise.

Examine whether these ideas have ever resulted in anything beneficial for you. Whether they are your ideas or the ideas of your family, society, philosophers, teachers or whatever it might be, examine where these ideas have led. Ideas about things don't lead to a peace of mind that is permanent. There is only one source for that, and that source is your very own open intelligence.

SUPERSEDING CAUSALITY

There are always button-pushing situations where our data get all riled up. Part of that whole process is blaming the people who have pushed our buttons, making them wrong and showing what a bad person they are, but that way of going about things is really very damaging to our well-being.

The moment that our buttons get pushed, that is the moment to immediately secure ourselves in open intelligence. Then, no matter what the data about the person or situation may be, we're secure in open intelligence. We really have to secure ourselves in open intelligence; otherwise, we'll continue to have our buttons pushed all the time.

There's so much discomfort within many people and so little idea of what to do about that discomfort. One's only recourse seems to be to insist that the discomfort is someone else's fault. One of the reasons that the world is in the state it's in is because of this insistence.

Human culture is diminished when we cannot get in touch with who we are and ground ourselves in that. We really have to see how grim it is in order to be willing to change the way we relate to ourselves and other people. It is not only the way we feel about other people but the way we relate to ourselves. If we can't see that there's something about us and everyone else that supersedes all of the data that are appearing, then we will get caught up in all kinds of cause and effect ideas about what's going on.

If we strengthen ourselves in open intelligence, then we supersede causality. What does that mean? It means that all the things that we thought had a cause-and-effect relationship aren't seen that way any longer. We may have thought that a certain person made us miserable, but to supersede causality means that we no longer see anyone as being capable of being the cause of our happiness or misery.

EASEFUL FAMILY RELATIONSHIPS

If someone is really established in relying on the alert, clear cognizance that is their own fundamental intelligence, then they can contribute beneficial circumstances automatically for many, many people. One doesn't have to try to figure out how to be beneficial to everyone. Quite naturally intelligence opens up into automatic benefit for everyone.

One example of the benefits of relying
is in family relationships. If one pe
established in alert, clear cognizance,
fortunate, because that single individu;
the family and then to everyone alto
people where there may have been lit
and the benefits of that sort of openness in ι·ι·.
enormous.

Many of us have difficulties in relationship because we're
often trying to make people do what we want them to do. We
think, "I'll feel good if they do what I want, and I won't feel
good if they don't do what I want." However, as we grow more
familiar with alert, clear cognizance, we see that this need not
be the case at all. People just are who they are, and that's okay.
By the power of relying on open intelligence there's a deep
connection and understanding that comes about, without having
to have people be or act any certain way.

Where we once had difficulty in relationship, increasingly we
find we have no difficulties. Where we once had a lot of
confusion about many different things, increasingly we have
less confusion, until there's no confusion at all.

SPEAKING WITH CONFIDENCE AND BOLDNESS

By relying on open intelligence you rely on that complete
confidence that's always present. In this way you are able to go
into situations that would have previously filled you with
anxiety and do exactly what needs to be done without fear or
apprehension. People are very convinced by what a totally clear
person has to say, because when open intelligence is relied upon,
the people who are hearing the message are put at rest, whether
they want to be at rest or not or whether they even know what
rest is.

get real with yourself, then you become a very [stron]g figure, and this is true for everyone. When you're [drawin]g on open intelligence, people want to hear what you have [to s]ay, no matter what you are talking about. They somehow know that they can count on the efficacy of what you are saying, because it is based in the profound insight of open intelligence. Even though they may not have known anything about open intelligence, they recognize it instinctively, and when you speak to them that recognition is part of the message people are getting.

There aren't any scripts to write; whatever is said is said without any thought of, "Oh, what are they going to think about me?" or "How is this going to make me look?" There is no referencing back to a personal identity. There is just the supreme boldness that comes from speaking with authenticity. In terms of the ongoing, practical everyday clarity of living a life, whether you are engaged with a large group or you are by yourself, there is a supreme boldness in every moment.

TRUE LEADERSHIP

If you need to appear a certain way to yourself or to someone else, you can't express true leadership. However, when you have unflinching courage, you don't need to appear any way to yourself or to anyone else. That is true clarity and freedom, and that is where true leadership and power come from. You can't be a truly trustworthy leader if you need to have all your thoughts, emotions and opinions approved all the time.

At some point you realize that neither your own thoughts, emotions and sensations nor those of anyone else can diminish open intelligence. It doesn't matter what other people are thinking about you or themselves—it need never affect your well-being. The only way to have the power to affect a situation in a way that will be mutually beneficial is through that kind of open intelligence. Otherwise, you're always trying to be a certain way that is predictable to yourself and to everyone else.

When you're unflinching, you're riding a tsunami of clarity and power that is not dictated by data. In being willing to hear about this amazing, effortless, unflinching freedom, a door is opened, and when you walk through that door, there is no turning back. There is the complete ease of being that brings an incredible shine to the skin and a smile to your face.

UNSHAKEABLE COURAGE

Whatever thoughts you have that are disturbing to you, whether they are past memories or fears about something that is going to happen in the future, the data stream is appearing right now! There is no future being lived out and there is no past you're hauling in. It's only right now. That's it; that's all you've got.

No matter how enormous and earth-shattering an experience may seem to be, you can't hang on to it. So, whatever data is streaming right now, it is spontaneously self-releasing. That's just the way it is, but to see this clearly you must make the commitment to being totally unflinching. When you meet someone who is unflinchingly committed to open intelligence, you know it. You can tell there isn't any wavering in them.

Whether you're a basketball coach, a composer, software engineer, scientist, politician or homemaker, the power of understanding the fundamental nature of your own experience will give you an extremely wide range of options for engaging in your work. You take the open intelligence of your experience and you integrate it into your chosen work. You rewrite whatever it is that everybody else had been doing. It doesn't mean that you have to completely do away with what has come before; it means that you see with total open intelligence what will work, and you have the unflinching courage to put that into form. With unshakeable courage you express the magnificence of your own being.

THE BEGINNING OF THE END TO ALL STORIES

Living a life based on conventional beliefs means that we will have an endless stream of stories in our heads that we have to sort out. For instance, a common story is that we are angry because someone said something we didn't like, and because of that we are in a bad mood, and because we are in a bad mood everything looks negative, and so on.

However, if that appearance of anger comes up and there is no story, then there is the ease that comes from not running a story. It is as simple as this: do we want the story and its roller coaster ride of emotional reactivity and compulsive thinking, or do we want to know the ease that comes from not going with the story? To experience the complete ease of not describing anything is the beginning of the end to all stories.

There is either the story or there is the recognition of open intelligence, but as long as there are stories and more stories, there is no clear recognition. But when we have complete certainty in open intelligence and no longer get lost in stories, there is a clarity that is absolutely stainless and clear like pure space, in which there is the simultaneous exhaustion of all the faults we've been trying to correct as well as the perfection of qualities.

To try to analyze and understand the stories through intellectual speculation will not give us ultimate relief. If we only analyze and speculate, then we get stuck in all kinds of conventional labels. One could continue to place meaning and significance in the stories that come up in the mind: "I don't want to fall in love because the person I'm in love with might not love me. I can't get the job I really want because I'm not good enough. I can't do what I really want to do because nothing ever goes right for me." But these stories only foster the restlessness of the mind. It's like being in a bubble bath with a mixer stirring up all the bubbles.

There is no need to apply antidotes to the flow of the stories. Work, alcohol, drugs, food, relationships and sex could be used as antidotes, but why bother with any of it? In the natural ease of open intelligence, everything we've ever wanted for our life and the power to skillfully express it will be found.

EVERYTHING COMES INTO ITS OWN PLACE

Negative thoughts, emotions and sensations may seem to be so strong at times that they are like an assault on our well-being. We probably haven't named the experience "an assault on our well-being," but in general there is a tone of anxiety or of something not being quite right that we carry around with us. This underlying or even overt anxiety comes from being out of tune with nature itself.

We don't want to live our life feeling like we are being assaulted by anxiety, and we use antidotes to relieve that anxiety so that we can feel better. We may have trained ourselves to think that when a discomfort arises we should do something or ingest something so that we can feel better. Most of us have quite a repertoire of antidotes that we concoct to deal with our discomfort, and the antidotes can become an addiction. We go to them because we have habituated ourselves to do so, and we come to depend on them.

We are kidding ourselves if we think we are going to get total relief through using an antidote. Sometimes we do feel better, but whatever the antidote is, it will not bring us increasing relief over time. We might think, "Wow, that cake looks so good; I'm going to eat as much of it as I can, and I'll feel so much better," or "I can't wait to light one up at the end of the day, and I'll feel so mellow then." We may return to the antidotes again and again, but we can never really rely on them, because they will never provide total relief from the discomfort.

We really have to see what we are up to in this regard and recognize that there really is a healthy alternative to taking an antidote: simply to rely on open intelligence and begin to become familiar with it as the fundamental nature of our being. It is much easier to habituate ourselves to identify with open intelligence than it is to habituate ourselves to all these antidotes.

The more certain we are of open intelligence, the more likely it is that we won't need the antidotes at all. But at the same time, there is no need to get into any kind of self-blame about all the antidotes we have been using. The focus has to be on short moments of open intelligence, many times—not on things we have been doing that we want to stop. If we truly see that these things are of no benefit to us whatsoever, we will naturally stop using them without even thinking about it, and this will come about in an easy way. I've seen it happen over and over again. Through the simple practice of short moments, everything comes into its own place in whichever way it needs to happen in our own particular life.

FLAWLESS OPEN INTELLIGENCE

We need to get to know ourselves as we really are and not be lost in our thoughts, emotions, and experiences. We need to get to know their underlying basis—that which is unalterable and unchangeable.

Most of us have believed that our thoughts and emotions exist in their own right, that they are a substantial entity and that they have a power to affect us. When we believe that, we are living in a very primitive way within ourselves, because we know so little about who we really are and so little about what our capabilities and capacities really are.

Our life may have been filled with all sorts of different emotional descriptions: sad, happy, grief-stricken, joyful or whatever it might be. We bounce around like a ping-pong ball between one emotion and another, always trying to make sense of them and giving them an actual power they do not have.

But indeed, whether it is an emotion or a thought or an experience we are giving power to, none of those exist in their own right. In other words, they have no nature that is independent of open intelligence. Without knowing that, we will constantly drift back to the description and the power that we believe the description has.

This misperception is due to not realizing that all of these perceptions appear within a crystalline space of flawless open intelligence. By gently relying on open intelligence rather than emphasizing the data that appear within it, the flawlessness of open intelligence becomes more and more obvious.

SOLUTION-BASED ORIENTATION

CHAPTER TEN

NO DISTURBANCE IN DISTURBANCE

Many of us have been at the mercy of our disturbing states for years and years. We have identified with them and suffered when they were intensely present. Short moments, many times cuts through that identification, and through the power of one's own experience it becomes obvious that there is actually no disturbance in disturbance.

As certainty in open intelligence increases and there is more certainty in natural perfection, there is a greater ability to see that data are more like friends or allies than foes or enemies. As that recognition becomes more certain in our own experience, soon there is no need for any thinking about data or any kind of response to them whatsoever.

When people hear about gaining certainty in open intelligence, they sometimes think that it means that disturbing data will disappear completely and will never occur again, and they'll live in a wonderful fairyland where there are only pretty pictures because open intelligence has overcome all the disturbing states! A short moment of the instinctive recognition of open intelligence reveals that disturbing experiences will continue to arise, but that we do not have to be mastered by them. When we see that clearly, then we can recognize self-arising wisdom as the disturbance appears. Gradually we come to see that all these disturbances are not disturbing unless we allow them to be.

By the power of certainty in open intelligence, it becomes clear that these data are self-releasing and are free in their own place. As there is no real disturbance in them anyway, there is nothing that needs to be done about them. As even greater certainty in open intelligence comes about, the data are seen to be completely empty of an independent nature. It's like going into a house that had seemed frightening and finding it to be completely nonthreatening. There is nothing there that can be found to be disturbing in any way.

Eventually the data are completely outshone by their own natural perfection. However, it isn't as if natural perfection somehow takes over and eliminates the data. No; we start to see that natural perfection is wholly present *within* the data. There never has been a division between data—phenomena—and naturally perfect open intelligence. By gradually recognizing this, what seemed to be two before, now is not. There is no two anywhere.

UNFLINCHING LOVE AND WISDOM

Life gets really interesting when all our buttons get pushed! Let's say we are with a friend, our partner, a family member or a work colleague, and they start doing things that annoy us. If we rely on open intelligence instead of going into one of our stories about what they are doing, more and more we will see clearly how to deal with a situation that may have caused us a lot of pain in the past.

Because we are so accustomed to reacting in some way when we get annoyed, at first it may be difficult not to react in this usual way. Through short moments many times, we come to recognize that there is a much more natural way to be. Rather than reacting based on habitual patterns of wanting to change, avoid, replace or micromanage the data, we rely on naturally responsive open intelligence, which is imbued with mental and emotional stability, keen insight and skillful knowingness of exactly what is needed. The more we do so, the more we realize that we do not want to go to that usual place of reactivity. We keep relying on open intelligence, and if action needs to be taken, we not only know what that action should be, that action will also be compassionate and beneficial by nature. This is very important and who knows where it will lead?

Sometimes people are a bit afraid when they hear something like this, and they think, "If I rely on open intelligence instead of reacting, maybe people will walk all over me." Well, anything could happen, but open intelligence has a natural discernment and stability, so whatever does happen, we are relying on the clarity of open intelligence and indwelling certainty in its powers of benefit, compassion, wisdom and skillfulness. We realize that we no longer need to react. We are unflinching in our love and wisdom without needing other people to be any particular way.

FOUR KEY POINTS

There are four crucial points to remember when emotionally heated situations get all stirred up: first, recognize that a datum is appearing and rely on open intelligence. So, there is recognition and acknowledgement that data are appearing. Second, allow open intelligence to remain *as it is*—open and spacious in the appearance of its own dynamic energy. Allow the datum, whatever it is, to come to its full potential. You don't try to suppress it or change it in any way. Let's say that you feel afraid; relying on open intelligence is not an antidote to the fear. It is the medium for allowing the fear to come to its full potential—hideous, glorious or whatever it is.

Third, see how the datum of fear vanishes naturally without a trace. This is how you come to see that there is nothing to be afraid of and nothing to hold on to either. The fourth key point is the stunning insight into this process of the simultaneous inception, full-potentiation and spontaneous release of the here-and-now. This most profound insight into this process of the resolution of data is the most profound insight any human being will ever have.

AT PEACE WITH OURSELVES

Whether we like ourselves or we don't, it really doesn't matter. Whether we've done good things or we've done bad things—or we've done a combination of the two—none of these are proof of our being an individual identity. We may have spent our whole life trying to shape ourselves into a good person, but we've never felt that we have attained that goal. Does that mean that we're a total failure and irredeemable? No, those labels are merely one more way that we have chosen to identify ourselves.

In each moment of open intelligence, all appearances are given their due. If we believe the history of everything that we have thought about ourselves, then we are bound to be very erratic. One moment we'll like ourselves, another moment we'll hate ourselves; one moment we'll like other people, another moment we'll have a litany of contempt going on about them. But by getting to know ourselves in a very thoroughgoing way, we see that our shape-shifting identity has never been anything other than clarity, love and tremendous energy.

If someone says to you, "You've got to get rid of the negative ego that's been causing you this trouble for all these years," then you can be sure that that person is not your true friend. Why? Because that advice will keep you on a hamster wheel, where you'll always be running after something that can never be attained. Do we want to put our attention on reforming an individual self, or do we want to recognize our true nature as open intelligence?

TREMENDOUS POWER AND ENERGY

The reason we get depressed, worried, angry, jealous or consumed with desire is because we're experiencing a tremendous amount of energy that we don't know what to do with. It's the energy of the basic state of natural perfection. When we relax our body and mind completely, that energy is completely released to be *as it is*, rather than it being described in all kinds of ways. Our natural disposition is to be filled with beneficial energy and to be able to proceed in the way that is most beneficial.

Our obsessive self-focus dampens down that energy, but by the power of instinctive recognition of open intelligence, the energy is released. The basis of everything is filled with tremendous power and energy. The true meaning of the word "empowerment" is to experience that energy and power decisively and directly as the very basis of one's own being. This is our own natural, beneficial state, our own natural, beneficial energy. It doesn't need to be cultivated or developed; it's already present. In the simple acknowledgement of it, it becomes evident, just like that.

FREE OF SUFFERING

Some of us have been depressed all of our lives, and we think we'll never be able to fully get out of the depression. But no matter what the appearances are or how gripping they may seem, when we discover the basis of those appearances—which is open intelligence itself—those labels don't stick anymore.

If we feel like we are really in the grip of something and we feel driven to act in a particular way to relieve our anxiety or depression, we can rely on that which is the complete relief of all anxiety, panic and depression—the relaxed nature of our being.

A lot of times we have been looking for tricks and gimmicks to get rid of our afflictive data, but these never completely work. Even if we find a way to drown the afflictive states for a while with a joint or a bottle of vodka, when these things wear off, what happens? The afflictive emotions come flooding back.

When we become familiar with open intelligence as the ground of depression, we see that the depression itself wouldn't exist without open intelligence. Instead of only knowing the one aspect of depression as something that we have suffered from and need to do something about, we discover the deeper aspect of depression—which is open intelligence. When we get familiar with open intelligence as the ground of the depression, we can maintain open intelligence in the face of depression with no need to alter or change what is arising in any way. We are no longer collapsed into this idea of ourselves as being a victim of depression.

We realize that in open intelligence we are really free of the suffering, even though there is suffering. This is completely beyond what can be understood in terms of dualistic thinking. Dualistic thinking says we are either suffering or we are not. But when we rely on open intelligence, we find out something much different. We find that what was afflictive before is no longer afflictive. This is how we come to see the power of open intelligence.

I am not saying that these afflictive states disappear. What I am saying is that, when we rely on open intelligence, we no longer see them as something that can alter our well-being. In maintaining unalterable, unchangeable open intelligence, it becomes more and more obvious to us that what appears in open intelligence, because it only is open intelligence, cannot alter or change open intelligence. No matter what appears, its appearance is a vivid appearance of open intelligence.

When afflictive states come up, it can be very difficult to recognize the natural ease of our own being, because everything in us is screaming, "No, no, this feels too awful. It can't possibly be part of open intelligence!" That's the most important time of all to just relax.

When we relax more and more, we begin to see that all the data that appear within open intelligence are our allies instead of our foes. When these appearances appear, we recognize inherent open intelligence. It could be that all of our lives we have been afraid of the afflictive states, but through open intelligence we are now able to see them as old friends. Afflictive states are a great support for relying on open intelligence; however, if we continue to exclude them as if they didn't belong in open intelligence, then we will be returning to them again and again.

If, for instance, we have a pain in the body and we're focused only on that pain, then that is all we'll see. But if we relax body and mind completely, then we can see this pain that is appearing is nothing other than an appearance of super-intelligence and flawless knowing. If we absolutely insist that we have a pain and it is *our* pain, then that's the only information we will have, and we won't be able to see it for what it truly is. But one thing is for sure about experiencing pain: it motivates us to look for relief from the pain. This is why afflictive states are our greatest friends. Without them we might never be moved to discover our ultimate nature.

When we get familiar with our ultimate nature, we just feel better all the time. There is no other way to say it; it's not a mysterious or esoteric matter. Our true nature doesn't belong to any kind of category, institution, philosophy or religion. It has never been owned by any country or by any person. We can either get familiar with it—or not. When we do get familiar with it, then we pass completely beyond cause and effect.

We see that all these appearances really are allies, and we have never been at their whim. It's all in what we take them to be. If we take them to be a monster, they will be. If we think we are ruled by them, then we will be. The more we know ourselves as we truly are, the more we see that we really are not affected by the labels we have used to describe everything.

LIONS AT THE GATE

Negative states are always with us, no matter who we are. They are unpredictable, countless and ceaseless and are part of the dynamic energy of open intelligence. At some point in our lives we may come face-to-face with an extremely afflictive state, and if we're lucky, we won't be able to ignore it! It will come up full force; there it will be, and we will be thinking, "Gee, I thought I could avoid that one, but now here it is again." Not only is it there, but we can't get rid of it.

These negative states need to be dealt with face-to-face as the reality of ourselves—not by ignoring them, not by trying to beat them into submission and not by trying to erase them from our experience. These afflictive emotional states are the lions at the gate of complete certainty in open intelligence. When these afflictive states come up, it might be very difficult for us to really see that they too are the face of open intelligence and nothing else.

When the afflictive states come at us full force, this is the time when it is really important to have support. Maybe we have already integrated all the positive and neutral data as open intelligence, but when we face these negative things, we see why we need to rely on someone who has integrated their own negative data as open intelligence and who knows what it is like to pass through the lions at the gate.

When the afflictive states arise with great vehemence, we have the choice to either go into them and be ruled by them or

121

to know ourselves as open intelligence. If we have difficulty in seeing that the afflictive states are nothing other than pure open intelligence, then that is a good time to seek support. We should go to people who have integrated their own negative data, because these are the only people who can truly help us.

Elizabeth!

CLARIFYING ANGER

Maybe in the past you have had situations where you got angry at someone and exploded at them, but afterwards you thought, "Hmm, maybe that wasn't such a good choice," and you felt really remorseful, or rather than feeling remorseful maybe you felt self-righteous indignation: "What do they know? They deserved it. I'm right." Whichever it might have been, it is clear that getting uncontrollably angry with someone is not a friendly or cooperative response to a situation.

We begin to see how these reactions have harmed us and harmed others. We see that recognizing open intelligence in the face of extremely negative data is a better alternative than acting them out. Even though we may not be able to stop these data from appearing, when they do appear we can at least see that recognizing open intelligence is a better alternative than exploding in anger. *the body took over, still does somewhat*

Let's say that something happens that has caused us to get very angry in the past. The real breakthrough of true open intelligence comes when we're right in the middle of the anger, and we really get it—firsthand and right away—that *everything* is included in open intelligence. When we can face anger or any other afflictive emotion squarely, exactly *as it is,* allowing naked seeing from within, that releases tremendous energy to be able to really see things for what they are.

Very strong data like anger are based on trying to defend and protect ourselves. What are we trying to protect and defend? Our self-styled individuality—which is what we take ourselves

122

to be. When we start to directly experience open intelligence and gain certainty in it, we don't have to figure everything out about why we do what we do. "Do I have a right to be angry? Can I be calmer so I don't get angry even when I have a right to be? Why can't I control my anger?" We give up reliance on intellectual speculation, and we rely on open intelligence alone. In our own experience we come to see that open intelligence is a better value proposition then any of our data.

compassion needs to take over. Anger is just energy.

TOTALLY FREE

There are many examples of people who have gained certainty in open intelligence, and so many of them report the same thing: it was their times of greatest adversity—whether it was war, famine, illness, financial disaster, loss of family and friends, terribly afflictive states—that increased their certainty in open intelligence the most.

There could be a lot of detours one could take; however, if the commitment is to open intelligence, then there aren't really any detours. Open intelligence is greatly comforting and provides a relief that is like nothing else. To rely on open intelligence is very self-reinforcing, because it's clear that to do so is much better than relying on data.

It's a lot easier to rely on open intelligence with the support of a trainer, a training and a community. Not only is it easier, it's also a lot more fun! If you really commit in this way, then very quickly you will recognize that open intelligence has been present all along but that you just hadn't noticed it.

Initially it's important to not be distracted by the negative states or perpetuate them by getting all wrapped up in your descriptions of them. As you gain more certainty in open intelligence, you could have the same negative state appear in full force, but you'd nevertheless be totally free.

You enjoy everything a lot more by not needing it to be any certain way. The ultimate freedom is in open intelligence, because from there you're totally free to be anywhere, in any situation and with anyone. You know what to do and how to act at all times. *all extreme statements that seem right but quite a leap—they don't talk much about process except over time you gain confidence in OI*

KNOWING THE SOLUTION

If you get scared, angry, desirous, jealous or if you think you are an idiot, the only resort is open intelligence. We all have feelings that come to us that we can't stop; we may think that we don't measure up or we are the greatest on earth or we are somewhere in between—but none of these self-assessments mean anything. Stay with open intelligence and everything will be seen for what it is. *I do this already.*

Social phobia, fear, panic attacks, anxiety and such things are actually normal responses to a life based on point of view, so don't feel you are abnormal if you experience any of these things. These are normal responses to a life based on describing everything, giving the descriptions meaning and trying to hold the descriptions at bay. By the power of open intelligence all of these kinds of fear are completely overcome. However, fearlessness can't come about by analyzing the mechanisms of fear or knowing more about fear. It can only come about through acknowledging the basis of fear, which is open intelligence. *I get it 2 get it, OK! 9-25-12*

All the while the fear and phobias that you have taken to be so powerful and to be something that can hurt you are what will set you free! Your very freedom lies in recognizing that open intelligence is the basis of all of these things. It would be impossible to even know what the descriptions of "fear," "panic" and "social phobia" are without open intelligence. *cool*

This is the significance of relying on open intelligence for short moments, many times as all these appearances come up in us. Short moments, many times may seem too simple or like it couldn't possibly work, but it is elegant and robust, and it will take you all the way to certainty in open intelligence. You can really count on that. By focusing on those short moments, you won't have to worry about the other stuff. It will completely subside. Just stay with what works.

Once you recognize open intelligence, there is no way to turn away from it. You can't go back to living in a fearful, anxiety-ridden and overwhelmed state. Once you know the solution, you definitely don't want to go back and live in the problem, because you've seen what the solution is. Even if you feel like you are not making any headway in relying on open intelligence, it doesn't matter, because you have seen the solution. *So true.*

We all want to be happy, and it's actually a very simple equation: open intelligence plus data equals happiness, because dat and open intelligence are equal. Believing that data are one thing and open intelligence is another thing is the crux of the problem.

As human beings we'll all go through the process of life: we are born, we live a life and then we die. One great master of *who?* open intelligence said at the end of his life with his face glowing with joy, "Oh yes, life is just one disappointment after another!" That's getting real. Life is one disappointment after another! We have wanted to stop our disappointing data, but that is a big mistake. The more disappointing, the better, because the more disappointing they are, the more likely we are to gain certainty in open intelligence.

hmmmm

That feeling that it has to be tidied up at the end — it's not true. It will just be what it is, + that's that! And that's ok.

125

THE TRUE NATURE OF MONEY

CHAPTER ELEVEN

A WHOLE NEW WORLD OPENS UP

Many people are worried about money, whatever their circumstances may be. Money is such a major focus because we have trained ourselves to misidentify what money is. We believe that money is the source of food, clothing and shelter as well as being the source of well-being. We think that we won't have well-being if we don't have money, and we think we will have well-being if we do have money.

The whole apple cart is turned upside down when we gain certainty in open intelligence. More and more we find that we don't think about money the way we used to. Money is no longer an obsessive underlying concern that rules our lives. Instead, natural perfection is seen to be the ground, and money is recognized to be just another datum.

If you really make a one hundred percent commitment to open intelligence, a world will open up before your eyes that will be like no world you've seen before. This can happen in many different ways, but as we have been talking about money, let's take that as the example. There might be a scenario where you were running out of money and had no evident means of getting more money. Then all of a sudden through some avenue that you could never have expected, the money that was needed came to you. You didn't really have to try to acquire it in any conventional way; it just became present for you without you having to do anything to get it.

When you live in a world made up only of your data about money, you live in a totally limited way. I cannot even convey how limited it is to live in that way. Real freedom comes with the complete resolution of the worries surrounding personal needs. You may have had ideas that getting your food, money and clothing was something you needed to be worried about, struggle with and focus on, but again, these are ideas that may not actually be true.

Maybe you have had to deal with lack of money your whole life, but then as you start gaining certainty in open intelligence, you might notice that these things that seemed so hard to get, for some reason, are no longer hard to get—but you didn't really do anything. All you did was gain certainty in open intelligence.

I'm not suggesting this as some sort of money-making gimmick or as a false hope program. I'm only saying that if you gain certainty in open intelligence your concerns about money, food, sex, shelter, clothing, work will resolve in the bright light of open intelligence. You will find that you have never needed to worry about any of these things.

You will also find that your valiant attempts to try to get all these things into your life are at best of secondary importance. These things are really not the places to invest your time or energy when it comes to understanding the purpose of human life and the potential of your own body and mind.

By gaining certainty in open intelligence, you gain trust in the fact that there is a fundamental way of everything being taken care of. All the concerns you had about where basic things would come from are released from being the center of attention.

OUR GENEROUS STATE OF BEING

Anyone who commits him or herself completely to open intelligence will find that open intelligence is a completely generous state of being. Our true identity is the naturally perfect basic state, and from the recognition of that it becomes possible to have a vital equanimity that pervades all experience. There is insightfulness, mental and emotional stability and skillfulness to be able to solve formerly unsolvable problems—whether they are personal or collective.

Total reliance on open intelligence can truly bring about a golden age where we are willing to share resources equally, and we are willing to engage democratically and cooperatively with others on a global basis. We also cannot govern or legislate equal sharing of the resources on the planet. This has to come from an innate peace and willingness to share.

If someone on the street came up to a passer-by and said, "I really need a jacket; please can I have yours?" the first reaction might be, "No, don't bother me," because the basic response of many of us may be to avoid situations like this or to cling to what we have. If we hold to this attitude, then we live life as a big "no" to sharing. But by instinctively recognizing the beneficial nature of open intelligence, it is possible to tap into the big "yes" within us that allows us to give generously and easily.

When we are asked to give, that is a wonderful opportunity to examine how we often contract and don't want to give. If we commit ourselves completely to open intelligence, we will find that open intelligence is a completely generous state of being. We can ask ourselves, "What is there to hold on to?" We can also come to recognize that giving can occur in many ways, not just through giving money or physical items.

When we gain complete certainty in open intelligence, all the concerns we have about where basic things will come from—food, money, shelter, clothing—aren't the center of attention anymore. We find that we don't need any particular thing in order to feel whole. We may have had the idea that we need to worry about our well-being in terms of food, money and clothing and that these are things to struggle over and that we need to spend our time, energy and attention focused on them in order to get by. However, the fact that we and many others have had this idea does not mean that it is actually true.

It might happen somehow that we could eventually get more money than we could ever spend; nevertheless, we know that banks and businesses have failed before and that they could fail again—just like they are failing now—and that getting and keeping money can never be fully relied upon. By being able to truly take this in, the strongly held beliefs we have had about money become less and less of interest to us.

When we rely on short moments of open intelligence, repeated many times, it allows us to loosen our involvement in trying to control all these data. Have you ever built a house of cards? The cards are placed carefully one on top of the other, but with a single breath they could all come tumbling down. To live in a house of cards is a very precarious and stressful way to live.

It is much better to commit to and rely on short moments of open intelligence and discover the beneficial intelligence of that. That will open up all kinds of new possibilities for making certain that we have a truly wonderful and abundant life.

MONEY, FOOD, RELATIONSHIPS AND SEX

When we live our life based on data, then we often seek identity in money, property and prestige. With money, property and prestige, the more we get, the more we want. It's a bottomless pit of persistent seeking for more. We often accumulate these things because we are looking for other people to acknowledge us so that we can feel like we are somebody.

The hoping for money, worrying about where to get more money, hoping that the money you have won't disappear or be taken away are often a great focus in life for many, many people, but has all the money you've gotten ever fully satisfied you? If you had all the money in the world, would that be enough? You could be in the position to say, "I have billions of dollars and I can do whatever I want; I can rule over everyone," but how long would that feeling be satisfying? Would even such tremendous riches bring peace to a rambling mind that's constantly dodging from one thought to the other?

If you love food, maybe sometimes you can't get enough of it and you just eat and eat. Over a lifetime that could end up being a mountain of food, but has any part of that mountain of food ever been fully satisfying? You have probably drunk lakes of beverages, but has all that drinking ever fully quenched your thirst?

Sex is another area of life in which people get very caught up. Say you had all the greatest kinds of sex in the world with gorgeous partners who were doing everything the way you wanted it. Would that really be as great as you've made it out to be in your own mind, and would you ever be totally satisfied?

Let's say you had everything you wanted in relationships, work, money, recreational activities or in the world political situation; is that going to ensure your well-being and make your life better and better over time? No. None of those things can offer you total well-being, because your well-being isn't in any of those things. Only your true nature can offer you well-being and total benefit that are present no matter what happens.

Once we know that we have within us the power to have complete well-being at all times, it's like finding the most precious gem that exists. When we find this most precious gem, we treasure and acknowledge it in every way and at every opportunity we can. When we discover this gem within ourselves, the benefits cannot be matched by anything else that life has to offer.

TRUE WELL-BEING

Do we live our lives in a way that we feel protected by how much money we have in our bank account? If so, we might think, "I've worked hard, I've put all this money away, I have good investments, my money will be there for a rainy day and this is what will sustain me." Well, with the financial crisis and the collapse of so many banks and financial institutions, that rainy day has actually come, and many people have found that the money they thought would be there for them isn't there at all. They thought they were living in a land of plenty, but that supposed land of plenty was a split second away from being a land of recession and hardship.

It's so important to get real about what's going on. We can't count on our data, because they will never bring us complete happiness and well-being. We also know we cannot count on our physical body, and we knew that from the moment we opened our eyes for the first time and took our first wailing breath.

Yet, even as strong as the fear of something like financial insecurity might be, the fear would vanish naturally without a trace if it were left simply *as it is,* without elaborating on the story that is spun out after the fear appears. But what happens instead is that when the fear arises, usually a story based on that fear arises as well.

For example, fear of financial insecurity appears and all of a sudden there is an immediate connecting of the dots with all the aspects of the story: the doubt about oneself and one's abilities, the lack of a job, the lack of money, the idea that we will suffer from this issue forever and so on. When the fear comes up, there really isn't anything to be said about it. One *could* say something about it, but that is not the optimal solution.

It is futile to believe in these stories. To keep seeking well-being in our stories and to go through decades of life seeking it and never finding it and continuing to seek for it—whew—that's exhausting! Why are anxiety, confusion and depression so epidemic? Looking in the wrong place for well-being, that's why. What is missed in all this looking for well-being is the complete mental and emotional stability that is right here, right now.

SOLUTION TO ALL PROBLEMS

It's very likely that for many of us the focus has been on acquiring the things we need in order to have a certain kind of life. In other words, we feel that we need to work hard to make money to provide for our wants and needs, and we spend quite a lot of time being concerned about money and trying to earn money to meet those needs. We are worried about whether we are going to have the amount of money we think we need in order to feel secure.

Even if someone has a large amount of money at their disposal and they don't need to work, there will still be concerns. Once we get so focused on these money concerns, money seems to be completely fundamental to our existence, and it's really hard to see it any other way. It creates a sort of blindness in us.

Some people are constantly looking for money, hoping for more money, worrying about where they are going to get the next load of money, hoping that the money they have won't disappear or be taken away. It may sound harsh to say so, but this is like what a drug addict does. A drug addict is always on the lookout for their next fix; they're worried that the drugs they have won't hold them long enough, and they're wondering where they can find the next connection to get more drugs.

I know people who have millions of dollars who are still worried about their money. They feel they don't have enough or they're not going to be able to hold on to what they do have. If they have children, they are worried that their children will not be able to deal with all the money that they will eventually inherit. If someone has that much money, taking care of it may end up being a great concern. So, if you've ever thought, "Oh, it would be great if I were a millionaire," know that there would still be data about money regardless of how much you had.

However, most people don't have the "being-a-millionaire" problem. For them the problem is at the other end of the scale: the zero-millions problem, meaning that they have very little money at all. They are worried about how to get food to eat, gas for the car, new shoes for the children and the healthcare that they need but can't afford. However, thinking that you are a millionaire or thinking that you are a zero-millionaire are just flip sides of the same extreme; your real identity is not found in either one of those descriptions.

Through holding to open intelligence, you open up to a whole new way of life. It is an incredible adventure when all of your experience—waking, dreaming, sleeping, being born, living, dying, abundance or lack—is attuned to your peaceful nature. That's where you're going to find the solutions to your personal problems, money problems and the world's problems.

A SPENDING LOG

One of the ways to get familiar with the way money really works is to keep a spending log. A spending log just shows you how you like to spend money. You keep track every day of the money you spend in different categories: personal things, business expenses, food, housing, entertainment, clothing, etc. At the end of the month you add up the expenses in each of these categories, and you see where you like to spend your money.

People like to spend their money on different things; there doesn't need to be any one way to handle money. Keeping a spending log is a good way to develop an excellent relationship with money. There are no limits on money, but unless one realizes that money doesn't have an independent nature, the point of view surrounding money will be limiting and restrictive.

If you're very thrifty or you're constantly spending more than you have or you're somewhere in between, at some point it would be beneficial for you to rely on open intelligence in relation to the data about money and all the stirrings it brings up. Money can bring up significant emotional disturbances, and when we're relying on open intelligence, we start to notice that. We ask ourselves, "Wow, I have these emotional reactions to money; what's that about?" We recognize the meaning and significance that we've given to money. To be able to recognize this comes from profound insight, and that profound insight can only come about through relying on open intelligence.

When we see that we've had inappropriate reactivity to something that has no independent nature—like money—then we can just relax. It doesn't mean that we stop working at our jobs, keeping track of our investments or that we disregard the fact that we need to eat each day. It just means that no matter what our money lifestyle is, we are paying attention in a very relaxed way.

Most people feel that money issues can make them or break them. In coming to completely rely on open intelligence with the powerful data of money, we'll find that, not only is this particular data resolved in pervasive open intelligence, but many other powerful data are automatically resolved as well.

When you find your peaceful nature in yourself, that experience can't be matched by anything in life. That's the greatest treasure you will ever find in life. There isn't anything greater. You could have all the money on earth, all the finest foods or whatever else you're looking for in the world, but it can't even come close to your peaceful nature. Your peaceful nature will take you all the way. When you are on your deathbed, your peaceful nature is the only thing that can sustain you. To go to your deathbed with the experience of peace is to be able to rest in peace and to die in peace. That peace is free of all the notions about everything.

By relying on open intelligence you make the best investment you can make. You make an investment with no downside and only an upside. You know that you've found what really works. When you see that all those things that you used to rely on are collapsing all around you and you still feel strong, peaceful, happy, and you want to reach out and help someone else—even though the world is falling apart—that's when you know that your peaceful nature is becoming more evident.

Anything can happen: banks could fail and you could lose all your money, the world economic markets could crash or the real estate markets could collapse. People think, "Oh, sure. That may have happened before, but it could never happen now." Yet, banks and financial institutions that people thought were untouchable have gone bankrupt. People lost millions and millions of dollars as the stock market plummeted and the financial markets of the world collapsed.

As we never know what's going to happen, we want to prepare ourselves with what can endure any experience. None of this financial unreliability is going to go away. We might as well breathe a sigh of relief and relax and get to know ourselves as we really are and discover the best means possible to deal with the circumstances that we will be facing.

Now, when a river flows, sometimes it rushes down swiftly, other times it flows over rapids and later in its journey it may flow easily and gently without any obstacles, but no matter what happens, the river keeps flowing. I could take as an example the Ganges River which flows out of the Himalayas in India. It flows out of a glacier high in the mountains, goes over waterfalls and through rapids and then eventually flows down to the plains. People are putting everything in the river along the way—trash, waste, filth, dead animals—and the river just keeps flowing, no matter what's in it or what obstacles stand in the way.

In a similar way, simply let all the circumstances in life do what they do. Our lives flow along in a natural way whatever the obstacles are, and all the while we remain grounded completely in the natural intelligence and peaceful nature that are at the basis of everything.

Whatever these situations are, there is nothing to be afraid of and nothing to hide out from. Why be afraid of what life will bring you? You're already rock solid. Rely on that which will carry you through any crisis.

REAL TRANSFORMATION OF THE WORLD

The world's economy has suffered enormous setbacks, and people are trying to scramble around using all the old ways of structuring an economy to get it back up on its feet again. New ways of structuring the capital markets will arise, and these new ways probably won't come from the people who created the old ways of structuring the economy.

The people of the world are finding out how much power they have, and in large part this has come about through the

Internet and telecommunications, where people now can gather together at the grassroots and create a groundswell for change.

As our existing institutions are crumbling, other institutions are arising. These institutions that are arising are fluid and flexible and are based on something entirely new. To say that these institutions are falling apart and there is a new way of understanding the nature of things doesn't mean that one collapses and then another arises. They are simultaneous. It is in the concurrence of the collapse of the old and the appearance of the new that there is a very powerful shift.

The greatest innovations in whichever field it may be will come from giving up the reliance on data and instead relying on open intelligence to find solutions to problems. It is a very exciting time, but the transition will be greatly hindered if we are trying to cling to our old ideas and ways of dealing with problems.

Rather than being distracted by all the terrific changes that are occurring in the world, it is important to root ourselves in open intelligence. That is what is going to carry us through to the end.

HAPPY AT WORK

You can be happy in your work by maintaining open intelligence, growing more familiar with open intelligence and by becoming more confident and certain in that open intelligence. By gaining more and more certainty in the essence of what you are, you will have the energy to truly be of benefit to everyone you come into contact with. Usually people don't go to work with that attitude; many people just want to do enough to get paid and then go home. But to go to work with the intention of benefiting your employer, fellow employees and everyone you meet at your job—well, that is a great reason to go to work!

By finding the complete comfort and relief within yourself, rather than relying on the descriptions—"angry, happy, sad, depressed, overworked, fed up with work, in need of a holiday"—you begin to see that there is no division within yourself.

It could be that things come up during the workday such as, "If I didn't have to work today, I could go surfing," or "If I had enough money already, I wouldn't have to be at this stupid job," or "I can't wait to go on holiday." Whether you're thinking "holiday" or "workday," both of these thoughts are equally insubstantial. It would be helpful to really look at what you might be putting yourself through by elaborating on these descriptions of holiday versus workday.

Where are those descriptions located actually? There isn't any place where a holiday or a workday exists as a substantial, independent thing that has power to affect your well-being. Do the concepts "holiday" or "workday" actually have the power to make you have a good or a bad day?

It's only through being trained in these beliefs throughout your life that you have come to believe that these ideas and emotions have a way to affect your well-being. To be beyond emotions does not mean to be emotionless; rather, in the arising of emotions you choose clarity rather than spinning out into an emotional state. You start to see that all of these events, emotions, thoughts and ideas don't have a power to affect the innate stability of who you are.

GIVING UP THE STRUGGLE

If you have been intensely competitive in certain areas of your life, such as in work, earning money, accumulating possessions and in athletic competition, by the power of gaining certainty in open intelligence you will lose the pleasure you have gotten from dominating and defeating other people. The desire to be better than others will disappear and it will be replaced by intense enjoyment of whatever you are participating in, whether it is athletics or business or any other area of life.

Rather than seeing someone as a competitor, it is possible to approach everyone with the balanced view of complete cooperation. There isn't anything separate from you; everything and everyone is an appearance within the basic state of open intelligence. When you gain certainty in open intelligence, you are completely grounded in this, with no need to dominate, control or assume a position of power over other people.

There is so much focus in our society on being the best, standing out, being famous and having more money than other people. Why not find out who you are and then see where it takes you in relation to all these other appearances?

When you train yourself in open intelligence, you train in excellent decision-making, you train in wisdom, you train in a balanced view and you train in seeing everything clearly. No matter whether you are ice-skating, playing tennis or engaging in business, science or politics, you are doing that with an effortless and balanced view. You may be engaged in intense activity, but that intense activity comes from a place of total open intelligence and ease. The intense activity rests in a fundamental basic state.

Look within yourself and say, "Well, who am I really?" and then let the discovery of that stand strong in your direct encounter with everything else that appears. Once you find out who you are and you train yourself in that recognition, all these other appearances really start to make sense, and they are not such a big deal anymore. No matter what happens in life, you have what you need.

This is what you really want in life: you want this sky-like balanced view. You do not want a competitive struggle with other people. The only thing that will take you through life easily is to relax and release your mind from the need to be involved in all these erroneous ideas, to release yourself into your basic state, to release yourself into open intelligence, to release yourself into a balanced view. The more you are able to do this, the less you will need to competitively struggle with other people.

ILLNESS, AGING AND DEATH
CHAPTER TWELVE

GREAT RELIEF

Aches and pains are part of having a human body, but to get all wrapped up in focusing on those aches and pains and trying to gain sympathy from others because of them can lead to a very gloomy life. Over the course of our life we learn to develop descriptive frameworks for the symptoms of disease, both psychological and physical, and it is quite easy to get caught up in what we could call "symptomatology."

I recently saw a little three-year-old girl, and she lifted up her foot for me to see and said, "Look! Look!" So I looked at her foot, and I thought that she was pointing to her new socks, so I complimented her on the socks. But she said very vehemently, "No, look at my ankle!" She pulled off her sock and shoe to show me the little scrape on her ankle, and she very much wanted me to notice it.

It is easy to see in small children how the focus on getting sympathy for aches and pains comes about. When little children fall down, one of the first things they do is to look to see how the people around them are going to react, then they often start crying and the adults usually respond with something like, "Oh, you poor thing!" This example could be seen as an analogy that illustrates the process of focusing on our aches and pains and attempting to gain sympathy for them.

When we focus on our psychological or physical symptoms, then it is possible that we will want to seek out other people who are focusing on the same thing. The moment we introduce our symptomatology into a conversation, we are potentially trying to attract a sympathetic response. We want someone to focus on our psychological or physical symptoms along with us, and that helps support us in believing that they are real.

But is this really the way we want to be greeting the symptoms that occur for us? Do we want to spend our time lost in symptomatology? Much better would be to gain certainty in open intelligence and see what all the aches and pains are about from that perspective. In gaining stability and certainty in open intelligence, we are able to see more clearly what should be done in regard to our psychological and physical symptoms.

If you do want support for what is happening for you, make sure you choose your support carefully. A person who is confident in open intelligence can support you much better than people who are all wrapped up in their physical and psychological symptoms. The people who are confident in open intelligence are going to be able to support you in the best possible way, whereas the people who are not living that way can't see anything else but psychological and physical symptoms.

If we can come to the definitive conclusion within ourselves that all our aches and pains rest in the basic state of open intelligence, that is occasion enough for a victory dance! We have great relief from the excessive focus on aches and pains, but at the same time we know exactly how to handle anything that may come up.

The symptoms are no longer anything that can make or break us, and we are no longer a helpless victim to whatever comes up for us. We can be warrior-like in the face of our physical and psychological symptoms.

ULTIMATE MEDICINE AND HEALING

In many countries people do not have the means for the kind of medical care that is available in the United States or Europe, either because they can't afford it or it isn't available at all. Many of the people around the world deal with devastating illnesses without having many options. They rely on folk medicine or palliative remedies or whatever might be available to them to carry them through to the end. They do not have access to the medical care or the medications they need, and they know that they probably never will.

People who don't have the money to go to the doctor or to buy medicine learn how to live a life that isn't dependent on that kind of care. They adapt the use of their mind so that they can live with whatever is occurring. Then, when the end comes after a long illness, they may never have gone to a hospital and they die very simply in the presence of people they've always known.

Many of us in the Western countries have the option of either intensive medical involvement or a simpler, less ordered way of leaving life. I am not necessarily saying that one or the other is the way that it has to be; I am only saying that we have a choice between those two. When we get clear, we see how we can decide what needs to happen for us.

Say for example you had cancer; if you choose to undergo many diagnostic tests and you get results that aren't good, then along with that negative result will be an avalanche of choices that need to be made in relation to that negative result—surgeries, chemotherapy, medications, more tests and more therapies of one kind or another. You could say, "Well, I'm going to go all out. I'm going to have all the tests, the surgery, the chemotherapy and the radiation." At the other end of the spectrum you could do nothing—or you could take other measures in between. It all depends on how you want to be focusing your energy and dealing with your physical symptoms.

Advertising, word of mouth and often the health care providers themselves lead people to believe that almost everyone is choosing the path of extensive medical treatment and that if you don't choose it you are the oddball. But the fact is that there are quite a few people who are not choosing to have extensive medical treatment, and with the baby boomers now getting into old age, there may be many more not choosing it.

So, you could choose a medicalized lifestyle or you could choose to do without medical care, but whichever it might be, you can also choose to put your focus on gaining certainty in open intelligence. If you proceed along with a course of medical treatment, then expect to have people treating you who aren't going to suggest that you engage stable open intelligence as the primary source of your healing.

By reaching for the ultimate medicine and healing of stable open intelligence, you will learn much about yourself and your own inherent stability. You can live an entire life with gracious, stable open intelligence that is exalted and beyond measure, and by the power of open intelligence you will see unmistakably what your choices should be in regard to serious illness.

WELL-BEING IN LONG TERM ILLNESS

When we are facing a lengthy and very painful illness, it is crucial to recognize that we need not be a victim of our condition. Well-being will come about through the clear seeing of our situation. We will not have well-being as long as we take ourselves to be a victim of what's going on with the illness. The fundamental illness that we in fact have is the mental instability that causes us to feel like we are a victim of the physical illness and the thoughts and emotions that come with the illness.

From open intelligence we can see what to do and how to act in terms of the situation that's going on for us. Even if somehow we found some kind of a cure for the physical illness, the mental instability would still be there—the basic instability whereby one perceives oneself to be a victim of one's circumstances. All of our ideas of being a victim of ourselves or of other people, places and things have to go out the window.

It is of course difficult to be facing a long term illness, but when people face extreme hardship, very often they are very clear about finding a skillful way to deal with the pain and suffering. They start to understand that seeing oneself as a victim of the suffering isn't necessarily the way that works best, and they begin looking for a way that does work.

No matter what happens as regards the illness, there is no medicine for death. What will sustain us at death is to gain complete confidence in the nature of our own being. To get familiar with that, we need to correct the fundamental misperception that thoughts and experiences are our enemy. If it isn't corrected, we will feel victimized to one degree or another.

If the physical condition changes for the better, that is fine, but we cannot count on that. Rely on open intelligence and come to know that this is something we can count on when dealing with illness. Have complete faith in the efficacy of just that.

SKILLFUL AGING

It's really important when we are getting older that we are totally clear about what's going on and what our choices are. What will be of greatest help to us when the body begins to fall apart and we know that we are eventually going to have to face death? Material possessions, wealth, security and acclaim will not be sufficient support to allow us to maintain open intelligence in the face of the emotional burdens, depression and the loss of physical ease and comfort that come with aging.

When we are young our whole life is in front of us. We are eager to make something out of ourselves in some way, and we live with that hope decade after decade. However, when we realize that this constant seeking to make something out of ourselves has come to an end, and we know that the body is aging and we are headed towards death, it can be very sad— even depressing. In fact, one of the greatest health problems for seniors is depression.

Early in life we have a strong physique, and if we get sick we bounce right back, but at some point that comes to an end and we don't bounce back. When we're young and we feel great and our bodies are functioning well, we think that we can get away with indulging, avoiding or replacing the data in order to try to improve our experience. But when we are old, we realize that our bodies and our minds are falling apart and the antidotes won't work as well. We're not able to indulge our physical desire like we once did, so we can't use that as an antidote. We realize that the condition of our body will grow increasingly worse with no possibility of avoiding or replacing unpleasant bodily states with a state that is more pleasant.

When it becomes clear that none of the antidotes will work any longer, people can become depressed. They feel depressed because they don't know a way out of these data. When there's no notion whatsoever that all the data can in fact be completely resolved in the indestructible basic state, then data can take hold in an older person more and more.

The only thing that can guarantee us that we're not going to be overwhelmed by what occurs late in life is to be rooted in intrinsic open intelligence. That's the best medicine. No matter what age we are, we can start right away with that medicine. Whatever the age, whatever the condition, whatever the opinion about the circumstance, the greatest stance is to be rooted in one's own intrinsic open intelligence and to gain more and more certainty in that.

What an adventure! We are never too young and never too old to gain certainty in open intelligence—we are always exactly the right age. Open intelligence never collapses into "young" or "old." It responds with perfect equanimity to everything that is appearing without any exception, all inclusive, all encompassing. This is the easy way to live.

FREEDOM FROM THE FEAR OF DEATH

It's really important that we gain certainty in open intelligence in regard to all the bodily sensations we will experience in life; otherwise, when we have illnesses, pain and unpleasant sensations we will get distracted by stories about them. It's really important to truly understand the nature of these sensations, because through that understanding we can develop a balanced view about what's going on with us.

The more we gain certainty in open intelligence, the more we see that we've had uncomfortable sensations all of our lives, but maybe we ignored them or glossed over them, because it would be overwhelming to allow ourselves to be with all these sensations. The reason we may have repressed or ignored these uncomfortable physical symptoms is that we don't want to face the fact that we're going to die. Well, guess what—we *are* going to die.

When we gain certainty in open intelligence, we can allow all the sensations—the comfortable ones, the uncomfortable ones and all the ones in-between—to be as they are. We uncover an incredible wisdom that has a totally balanced view. It's only in that balanced view that we really can choose options and alternatives that will serve us and serve others completely; if not, it is very likely that we'll get sucked into a story about whatever symptoms we are experiencing.

When we allow all of our bodily sensations to be as they are, then we come to understand the datum of death and are less afraid of it. In my own experience in gaining certainty in open intelligence, this was one of the very initial fruits of the practice.

After a life filled with foreboding fears of death that got me lost in all kinds of incredible stories, the fear disappeared completely—never to return.

By really encountering this fear of death in the practice of short moments many times and just allowing all the fear to be *as it is*, you are able to have complete relief from the fear of death. This relief can come swiftly and surely or it can come slowly, but whatever way it comes, please allow yourself to gain certainty in the utter lucidity of open intelligence in the direct encounter with these data. By doing so, when you are dying, you will be able to easily rely on that lucidity, and all the accompanying data of being a somebody will resolve. All there is, is the utter lucidity of open intelligence.

READY FOR DEATH

There is no getting out of death. That is self-evident, but many of us are trying to side-step dealing with death because in an unconscious way we imagine that somehow life will just go on and on. So, it is very important to come to terms with the fact that death will come; it cannot be avoided and we have no idea when it will come. It could come at any moment, so in the face of a health dilemma the priority about our actions should not only be, "How am I going to solve this temporary health crisis?" but also, "How will I meet my death which could occur at any moment?"

The present moment is the right time to begin relying on open intelligence, regardless of how old we are or what our life situation is. At the same time, when we are young, healthy and strong, that is an opportune time to rely on open intelligence, because the more we age the more there will be the demands of the physical body, emotions and thinking, and the more our energy will be sapped by the aging process.

We all die of the same thing—death. If we really want to be ready for death, then that's going to come from realizing that all phenomena whatsoever—including death—are the dynamic energy of open intelligence. To see that all phenomena are included in open intelligence is very freeing. When we have complete certainty in that recognition, we live life afraid of nothing.

HAVING A PLAN FOR DEATH

We should have a plan that accounts for the fact that death can come at any moment. That plan is to gain certainty in open intelligence right now! We should also have a practical plan for what we will do if we receive devastating news about our health. For instance, we may get a diagnosis that we have heart disease and we need open-heart surgery, or we may find that we have cancer and we have six months to live. We are told that we have the options of surgery, radiation and chemotherapy and that we need to decide very soon what we will do.

We should have a plan about what we're going to do before we ever hear that news, whether we use the plan or not when we get the news. This is an expression of the balanced view of wisdom. This will save us a lot of grief, and it will save the people around us a lot of grief.

If we don't have that plan, not only will we be hearing shocking and startling news, but we'll also be hearing all sorts of proposals and suggestions surrounding that news that we've never had to deal with before. These are likely to be matters that most of us don't know much about, so we might not be able to fully understand what our options are.

In a very practical sense, what would that detailed plan look like? It would involve delegating a medical power of attorney and having other legal instruments in place that indicate exactly what should be done. The people who are part of that plan should know the details about it and should have agreed to it. Additionally, one should have one's household affairs in a condition such that our death would not be a great burden to others. In other words it should be clear where the possessions will go once the person has died. There should be a will that has been drawn up with clear direction in terms of a funeral and whether there will be a burial or a cremation. If everything is laid out so completely, then no one else has to do anything except execute what's been planned.

With wisdom we know exactly how to organize *all* of our affairs, including the practical affairs in our daily walk of life: financial and business decisions, our relationships with food, work, friends and family, our love life, our social life, and whatever else it might be. Through short moments repeated many times we come into true open intelligence, compassion and wisdom in which we uphold our own naturally occurring dignity and integrity. That way we can be completely beneficial to ourselves and others.

THE PROCESS OF DYING

If we haven't become convinced of our own mortality, by the time we're around sixty our mortality is going to come calling! Once the body starts to fall apart, the mind may also start to fall apart, and then all the strategies that have been put in place for controlling the mind won't work. Even if we're able to get them to work now and again, when we're on our deathbed, they *definitely* won't work, because the mind gets all fuzzy and confused. If we've been doing positive affirmations, we're not going to be able to do them anymore. Even if we could do them, they would seem extremely hollow. We'll be too confused to drum up, "I am alive and well," and to be saying, "I am rich and famous" on our deathbed would be pointless.

In the process of death our whole way of perceiving everything completely breaks down. If we have felt that we were in control all of our lives, we won't feel that way at the time of death. Everything starts shutting down. The seeing gets fuzzy, we can't smell or taste anything anymore, and when we try to touch something, we can't really feel it's there. We can't feel the warmth of the skin of our loved ones. Our hearing starts to fade out. We can feel our heartbeat getting weaker, and our breath gets shallow.

We lose any sense of being able to feel emotion about anything, and we lose our ability to think about anything. When we are dying we don't have the ability to conceptualize any longer, so the whole point of view of "my life" begins to disappear as though it never was. That can be very frightening if we've thought that "my life" was essential to our identity.

In the moment of death everything goes completely haywire. Most of the time the dying person can't say anything to the people around them, but they are thinking thoughts like, "Oh my god, what's going on? I never thought it would be like this. This is really scary. I'm probably never going to eat again or have a drink of water again. Pretty soon I'll take my last breath."

When we are dying, we are in a completely different world of data from the people around us who have no idea what we are going through. It's easy to be pretty anxious in a situation like that, but if we prepare ourselves by deeply understanding the fundamental nature of our own condition, death will be just another here-and-now. There won't be any writhing and tweaking—or even if there is writhing and tweaking—we'll be completely relaxed and at ease. By the power of instinctive recognition we look everything right in the eye.

When we look death right in the eye, then we're no longer afraid of it. Every here-and-now, whatever it is—no sight, no hearing, no taste, no touch—is just fading away. By the power of instinctive recognition, we are as we are, right here and now.

WHEN WE DRAW OUR FINAL BREATH

Even though we will all die some day, it isn't open intelligence that dies. Our phenomenal appearance may change, but it only changes within the continuous flow of open intelligence—what it's always been anyway. When we recognize that the indestructible basic state of open intelligence is the basis of all of our appearances, including our death, then we can have an easeful death because we're not looking at our death as being a separation or an end.

It isn't that we need to think this through and convince ourselves; we instinctively realize that death is merely another data within open intelligence that has been labeled as something and then given significance based on the definitions of the perceiver.

By the power of instinctive recognition of the basic state of open intelligence, it's realized that the fundamental definition of death is the indestructible basic state—just as the fundamental definition of birth is the indestructible basic state and the fundamental definition of all of life is the indestructible basic state.

To have the precious opportunity of finding out about open intelligence is not something to be taken lightly, because the instinctive recognition of open intelligence is what will allow us to die in total peace.

A BEAUTIFUL DEATH

When we think about death, a *beautiful* death isn't usually what comes to mind. We have many thoughts related to death, and we hope that we might avoid a difficult death, but many of the ways in which we've been introduced to death don't support us in feeling that we can have a *beautiful* death. We primarily learn one of two things: one is that when we die, if we've been good we go to heaven, but if we've been bad we go to hell. The second belief that many people have is that when we die we will be reincarnated according to our karma, and we will get another lifetime in which we hopefully can have a better life.

When we live under the pall of data such as heaven and hell or karma and reincarnation, then we feel very restricted in our life. We feel that death is the final assault on us as a "somebody." Our life will end and it is this enemy—death—that will take it away. If we don't view death as an enemy, we at least view it as a foe, but the only reason we do so is because we don't really understand what death is.

It's really important for us to realize that this death that we all will face is very much something that we can become acquainted with in life. How do we become acquainted with it? By knowing who we are. Gradually we become familiar with ourselves as the timeless nature of open intelligence that is the space of all data, including the datum of death.

When we live our lives with great diligence as timeless open intelligence, we have the great fortune of knowing that we are free. We no longer have the concerns of the body, and all the restrictions of our body vanish naturally. We're very clear that the body is a datum and that it's not the basis of who we are. We see that the substance of who we are is open intelligence, which is the great reality of everything. Then, even though we're still experiencing a body, we become acquainted in a very real way with what will sustain us at the time of death.

Rather than feeling confined to the body, we feel more like the space inside a vase or like the waning moon vanishing into the expanse of the sky. Our practice of growing familiar with this as the true reality of who we are in life is what prepares us for a beautiful death. This is the great reality of ending our lives: we become the timeless open intelligence that we've always already been. That timeless open intelligence is entirely empty of being anybody, yet at the same time it is naturally present as everything.

Death, rather than being something to be feared, is something that we can embrace. What more intimate way is there to be with ourselves and to be with each other than to serve each other in having a beautiful death.

always + already = adya says a lot.

Section Four
Open Intelligence in Relationships

FINDING LOVE
IN ALL THE RIGHT PLACES

CHAPTER THIRTEEN

PURE LOVE

Valentine's Day is certainly a day that is filled with very high expectations! We want to do the right things for our romantic partners, and we subtly hope that they will do the right things for us. We want to be acknowledged by our loved ones, and if they don't acknowledge us, that may be disappointing. Whether it is from our significant others, our friends or in what we expect from the day itself, in a subtle way we want flowers to rain down on us! This is a silly and absurd example, but it is helpful to see how we expect love, affection and approval from our outer circumstances.

Through relying on open intelligence and growing more confident in it, we find ourselves more capable of loving ourselves and loving others. We reach a point where we don't demand anything from anyone else, because we know that ultimately there's nothing that anyone else can give us. We abide in a state of pure love where there aren't any expectations placed on anyone for anything. It is all the same whether anyone shows love to us or not.

Pure love doesn't have any need for anything—it just is *as it is*. This is what open intelligence is: the all-inclusive intelligence that doesn't need to have data be any one way or the other. It inherently knows—without knowing anything—that everything is itself. Everything is the self-display of this love; there is an embrace of the complete love that is the basic goodness that we are. This is what we're all looking for when we are seeking for love and affection in outer circumstances.

157

There's nothing to grab on to in the spontaneous release of the here-and-now. When we grow more familiar with the way things really are—rather than wishing they would be some certain way—we move beyond the constant seeking for fixed reference points. Even if thoughts of disappointment come, we see that they are merely circumstantial appearances that have no bite, and for that reason disappointment is no longer part of our lives. This is a very relaxed way of being that is saturated with empathy and sympathy.

ENGULFED BY TRUE LOVE

A big idea about love is that there is love only when it is associated with an object. For example, "I love *you*; I love that *place*; I love that *thing*," but that is not where love is located. Love is located in its own place. If we can recognize this, we will no longer need to be involved in the cat and mouse game of seeking and finding love in all manner of data, having it slip away and seeking and finding it again.

By taking short moments of love, we see so clearly that our only identity is the unconditioned love inherent in open intelligence, and everything that appears is a sparkling emanation of that love. We can engage life with completely carefree openness without limit. In this way we can live in a very relaxed, warm and direct way and naturally be of benefit.

When we are engulfed by true love, whew, it's all over! All the misapprehension comes tumbling down without any effort at all, and all that's left is the love that is always present. Why would it be necessary to have some kind of tangle of words to make sense out of it? Would sorting out the tangle need to be the project of an entire lifetime? The heart call of every moment is forever unencumbered and incredibly precious. The nature of love is this simple heartfelt attitude that penetrates every thought, emotion, sensation and experience. Once the alarm of love rings, there is no way to ignore it.

There are many things that can seem to comfort us in many ways, but there is no person, place or thing that we need to keep in place in order to ensure our ever-present well-being. Our ever-present condition is the natural perfection of everything. There is nothing to seek; where we are is where we always are—resting in our authentic condition. What is most basic in everything is completely native, naked love.

TO LOVE AND BE LOVED

The impulse of human life is to love and be loved. When we are very clear within ourselves about what that love really is, then we come to realize that everything about us is an expression of perfect love. This is true for everyone without exception. Love isn't dependent on pleasurable people, places and things. Love is already present, and everything depends on it.

Love is pure—which means it's free of anything of a different kind. Everything that arises, arises in love, as love and through love. It will never be any way other than that.

The enlivening of love occurs in each moment. Love lives in every one of our experiences. Whether we experience pleasant or unpleasant thoughts, emotions, sensations, love is the force within it all. Everything is a self-presentation of love and the self-sound of love. There is absolutely no exception to that whatsoever.

In every moment of everyday life, that's where we recognize pure and perfect love. It isn't anywhere else. What shines forth from within the wild swings of every single thought, emotion, sensation and other experience is the great singularity of pure and perfect love.

First and foremost we must realize that we are the ever-presence of pure and perfect love itself. We don't have any identity that was ever split off from that. We are the center of love radiating out as everything that appears. Love is evident in our own awareness of everything, so everything we see, taste, touch, hear and smell is the self-presentation of love. All speaking and all thinking are an expression of love. Our different emotional states are pure and perfect love. There isn't a need to go anywhere for love, because love is already present. Love isn't conditioned by special circumstances of any kind. No matter what the circumstances are, they are the circumstances of perfect love.

As everything is bound by love, there is no way to get out of love. Love is always flashing forth in every single experience, whether we recognize it or not. This might go against everything we've ever thought, but when we no longer take ourselves to be the appearances, then we really know that we are the expression of pure and perfect love. This is enlivened in every moment in the actual conduct of our life. It is a lived reality.

The natural heart-warmth that we feel and express in every moment of living is evidence of love. Within ourselves we find that pure and perfect love is perfect insight in all circumstances, complete mental and emotional stability and skill in all circumstances. It is profound compassion, which means that every moment of life is an expression of sympathy and empathy. Its expressions are far-reaching. Everyone is already in touch with it, because that's all anyone is. It is impossible for it to be hidden or obscured.

Love can never be limited by an idea. The expression of love can be peaceful in one moment, and it can be entirely wrathful and freewheeling in another moment, but whichever it might be, its expression will be of profound benefit.

The basic state of everything, just *as it is,* is inseparable from precious life itself, and to try to retreat into any corner of life in order to find love there is like sky trying to retreat into a part of sky to find sky.

As long as we're continuing to push things away or pull things towards us, we'll never have the instinctive recognition of love in life. Give up all effort whatsoever to change any appearance. Even if you're really good at arranging appearances, in the end it will all be for naught. If you are running from one experience to another in search of love, you are looking for love in all the wrong places. What is important is that everything is recognized as arising in love.

The idea of loving and being loved is so compelling to all of us, and we long to share and enjoy love with other people. The only way we are going to be able to truly share love with other human beings is by recognizing that we have never been anything other than love itself.

People like to hear about love, but the word lacks an accurate definition. Many times we have an idea about love and we think, "Oh yeah, I know what that is." For instance, we have the idea that love needs to look a certain way, or that we will only have love if we are nice to other people and earn their love, or that they need to be nice to us to earn our love. It is in realizing that there is no need to regulate life that love becomes the real force of one's life.

The swift and sure introduction to love is found in the total pure presence of what is right here. There is no need to seek it, find it or put anything in place to ensure it. By the power of short moments we realize that we are forever swept up in the swoon of love! All the illusory ideas about what love is disappear completely.

Living the life of true love—even if you are the only one who seems to be living it—is exuberant, exciting and a great deal of fun. If you are so fortunate to share that with another person, then your life is very privileged. By knowing your own nature, you automatically know the nature of everyone, and knowing the nature of everyone is what it means to love unconditionally.

LOVE IS ALWAYS PRESENT

I can share my ideas about love with complete conviction, because I have found them to be true in my own life. I am not talking about a philosophy; anything that is suggested here I have found in my own experience. What I thought from the beginning of my life—that everything is an expression of naturally perfect love—I have now found to be true. Wonder of wonders!

Love is so all-giving, all-pervasive, all-wondrous and all-sublime, and absolutely everything is included. When we realize that we are an expression of love, we see that love wholesomely unites everything. In our own experience we find that everything is wondrously unified in perfect love. We don't need to try to be nice to other people, and we don't need to aspire to have healthy relationships—those things occur automatically. We are happy to know the people around us and share life together with them in a truly intimate relationship that doesn't need to look any special way.

Love is totally out of control, but in fact we wouldn't want it any other way. When we are able to know that love already is *as it is* and always will be, then we live life in a completely relaxed way, because we automatically know that we're going to be able to respond with true connection no matter what situation appears. Gone are the days when we feel that we need to figure out what to do and spend days plotting out circumstances to create some clarity out of the confusion.

Love is always present, and its truly sublime skillfulness cannot be equaled by any conception of what to do or how to act. Love is a spontaneous heart-burst of perfect expression that's present in all situations—in living life in a totally ordinary way, sharing with each other with complete openness and being willing to plunge into all experience with confidence.

Everything all at once is wholly positive. All-at-once-ness is the expression of love's force. Whether the expression is of a pleasurable thought or one that is horrible, whether life is seen as boring, dull and passive or as ecstatic, we deeply recognize in ourselves that all of it is the perfect expression of love.

There is never any need to wonder as to where love is. When we find it, we see that it is completely empty of anything else other than itself. It is naturally present, and its true love force is one of perfect responsiveness in all situations without exception.

TREMENDOUS POWER, ENERGY AND LOVE

If you're walking down the street and you see someone behaving in an odd manner and the thought comes, "Look at that person over there. Why do they have to act that way?" just know that everyone, no matter who they are, is absolutely yearning for love. They're yearning for a sense of connection with everyone and everything, and that's the only reason anyone does anything. We're always searching for that love and sense of connection. To recognize this completely changes your perspective, and you can see yourself and everyone else in a new and profound way. It is possible for you to see how many people there are who are burdened with fear and loneliness.

If you have little fears or big fears, why continue to focus on them as being *your* fears? They are the fears of *all beings* appearing in the immediacy of the here-and-now, and they've never been limited to being an isolated fear occurring for one individual. It only seems that way if that's what you believe.

It can perhaps seem overwhelming to be alert to all the fear and suffering that are taking place around you. However, in doing so and allowing your own natural blissful compassion to be present, you discover a tremendous power, energy and love that you may never have noticed before, but which were always present.

TRUE INTIMACY

When we take ourselves to be a biological and psychological subject made up of data, we are likely to be in competition with others who we take to be biological and psychological objects that have their own data. We substantialize ourselves with our own data and substantialize others in the same way. We do this in so many arenas of life: in our families, in our intimate relationships, in the workplace, in social and political organizations, business, everywhere—substantializing ourselves with data and comparing ourselves with and competing with others.

We never have any true intimacy in this way—not with ourselves or with anyone else. How can we have intimacy with someone when we are always trying to defend and protect our data and show them that their data are wrong and need to be changed? If we believe that we are an accumulation of our historical data and we believe that other people are as well, then there will be two accumulations of data relating to each other—sometimes coming together easily but sometimes being at odds with one another.

To realize that no appearance has an independent nature is to free ourselves to love our own appearance and the appearances of others as well. No longer are our thoughts about people, places and things collapsed into a state of un-love. Instead, we are receptive, sparkling and free in a simple human way.

164

We are completely open to enjoy whatever the appearance might be, whether it's our next door neighbor, our wife or husband, the shopping mall or the splendor of the natural world—it's all equal. It is all a free display of open intelligence. The only way that we can really recognize that is in our own experience. If this recognition of reality takes hold, we see that we have never been captured in any way. We have always been love, and that has never been captured by any appearance.

LOVE-FILLED

One thing I learned very early on was that everyone wants to love and be loved. I also learned that everyone wants to belong, in other words, to not be ostracized or set aside by others in any way. The third thing I could see was that everyone had tremendous gifts to give, and it was through love that these gifts would be recognized and contributed. I knew these things, but I didn't really know much about practically applying them until I was much older. But wherever I went, I looked at what I saw in those terms.

It was interesting for me as I grew up, because I saw that the institutions I was involved in—schools, churches, businesses— were not organized in the way that I had understood things. In fact, they were organized as structures of fear, based on the idea that, if you didn't toe the line and behave according to expectations, you wouldn't be loved, you wouldn't be allowed to belong and you could be sent away. How would a person be able to find his or her strengths, gifts and talents in an atmosphere like that?

From the time I was young I had a deep belief that if people got familiar with love, all of the things I had wished for would become possible. If we knew ourselves as love, then our families, communities, institutions, countries and our world would become love-filled.

I have stayed with this belief until it became an actuality, and I know now that it is true. As one of many participants in this worldwide Great Freedom and Balanced View organization, I know that it is possible to have organizations that are filled with love and caring, where everyone is mutually supported to succeed.

ROMANTIC AND SEXUAL ATTRACTION

CHAPTER FOURTEEN

not vital sexual energy — as Ken W. talks about it's "whole" energy.

THE TRUE NATURE OF SEXUAL ENERGY

At some point in our lives the sexual urge awakens in us, but we are never taught that this energy that we label "sexual" is in fact the life force of connection, intimacy and compassion. It is important to really understand this. When we gain more certainty in open intelligence, we begin to see that what we call sexual energy is always present as the energy that pervades everything that is. It is not something that is merely localized in an individual or in the pleasure that seems to be limited to sexual expression. Sexuality is really the life force of connection with everyone and everything that is naturally inherent in open intelligence, so never be confused about that.

Typically what we know about the expression of our sexual nature is that we want to get together and have sex with someone else whom we find attractive. There will be certain people we like to have sex with and others that we don't. When we want to have sex, then we seek it out, and once we get it, then we will want to keep having it and have ever better versions of it. Yet, no matter how good the sex is, it will never quite be all of what we want it to be. So, then we think we have to make it better, and this keeps us in this tailspin of never feeling quite fully satisfied.

There have been times in our lives when we have been sexually attracted to certain people, and sexual attraction can become a powerful point of view. We have all these imaginations about what it would be like to be with that person, and we are scheming different ways so that we can be with them and act upon some of this fantasy that we've got going on.

When we are no longer driven by all these data, we start to see the nature of sexual energy very clearly, and we are no longer driven to express it in a way that follows this pattern.

Whether we are having sex or not, any circumstance is the perfect circumstance for relying on open intelligence. Relying on open intelligence has never been bound by any conventional designations, because it is the root of all conventional designations. When we rely on open intelligence for short moments, repeated many times regardless of circumstance, we begin to definitively realize that we are not dependent on anything. If we continue to think that we need to have certain conditions to enable us to rely on open intelligence, then we have instantly created more duality.

We may think, for example, that we are not going to be a good enough person to recognize open intelligence unless we are expressing our sexuality in a certain way—such as being celibate or not having sexual thoughts—but this is just another designation that is being applied to open intelligence, and open intelligence isn't bound by anything.

If you want to have an incredible experience of coming together with someone in a sexual way, it is going to require that both you and your partner be confident in open intelligence and really understand the purpose, meaning and import of your sexual nature.

ROMANTIC AND SEXUAL ATTRACTION

There probably isn't any person who has not experienced sexual attraction towards someone else at some point, and that remains true even if one tries to hide from or do away with sexual feelings. Whether it's indulged or renounced, sexual and romantic attraction is still present and ready to appear at any time. By the power of gaining certainty in open intelligence and allowing ourselves the space to let everything be *as it is*, we can clearly see the dynamics of sexual attraction. If we don't allow ourselves the space to see the working of this dynamic energy, then we'll never have the complete resolution of the data that surround sexual attraction.

When we begin to allow sexual and romantic attraction to be *as it is*, we may notice that we have all kinds of sexual attractions that we never thought would appear. We might find ourselves being sexually and romantically attracted to all kinds of people whom we would never have allowed ourselves to be attracted to before, because we would have suppressed the attraction. This random sexual attraction is no cause for alarm or fear. If we rely on open intelligence, we get to see how dynamic the display of romantic and sexual attraction is, and we understand how not to be caught by it.

When we experience romantic and sexual attraction for a particular person, first of all there might be a thought like, "Oh wow, they're hot!" and there might be all kinds of images that appear along with that impression. All of a sudden there is a surge of emotions, thoughts, sensations and fantasies about the experience we could have with that person. We have our fantasy images of what it's going to be like, and we either act on them or we don't. If that's all we know about the flow of the dynamic energy of sexual data, then we'll be completely lost in the story that comes with all the thoughts and emotions.

If we don't learn about the nature of this dynamic energy, we cannot have a full and complete sexual and romantic relationship with another person. The thing we want—to have a good sexual and romantic relationship with someone—is what we cut ourselves off from by not gaining wisdom in this extremely important matter.

Once we are able to maintain open intelligence in the direct encounter with those data streams, then we see that we really are attracted to many people in many different ways. To see that there really isn't any "special someone" for us gives us much greater freedom in terms of who we will choose to be with, if in fact we choose to be with anyone in a romantic way.

If we see that sexual and romantic attraction or having a romantic partner is not necessary to our well-being, then we have complete freedom as to whether we will have a sexual relationship or not. If we choose to not have a relationship, it won't be because we've cut off or renounced our sexual feelings and sensations. Through understanding the dynamics of sexual attraction completely, we come into an authentic relationship with whomever we choose to be with.

TOTAL PLEASURE

Most of us develop very ambivalent belief systems about our sexual nature. What that means is that we love sex, but at the same time we have all sorts of conflicting ideas about it. We may have learned that only certain kinds of sexual lifestyles are appropriate, or that sexual relations should only occur in a monogamous relationship, or that one should not engage in sex before marriage, or conversely, that anything is allowed as long as it feels good. We may have also learned to be troubled by the sexual fantasies we have.

Over time we absorb a belief system from the culture in which we have grown up, and that cultural belief system is quite possibly present in us in a completely unconscious way. The more of these belief systems we acquire, the more ambivalent we feel about our sexual nature. We may hear all sorts of different ideas about sex from many different sources, but that doesn't really resolve the ambivalence about sexuality. The sexual movement that we feel in the body isn't always interpreted in the same way by all people, nor do we always interpret it in the same way for ourselves. We circle around in these many belief systems without having a clear notion of what the energy in us actually is.

The more we release our hold on these strict belief systems, the more complete we feel about ourselves and others and the more understanding we have for ourselves and others. If we rely on open intelligence while exploring our sexual nature, we have the direct experience of the reality that our sexual nature is nothing other than open intelligence itself and that there is no reason to be ambivalent about our sexuality. We come to really see that all of these thoughts, emotions and sensations of the body are an expression of open intelligence. But if we mix the thoughts, emotions and sensations together and make a decision about engaging sexually only based on them—without recognizing their essence as open intelligence—there won't be clear seeing.

Come to know this wonderful expression of human living *as it is*. It is an expression of open intelligence; it is not something to be avoided—but neither is it something to be expressed uncontrollably. The expression of the sexual nature needs to come from clarity, not from uncontrollable desire. When we rely on open intelligence, then right action ensues. We know what to do in an unerring way without thinking about it, and what we do is beneficial to ourselves and others.

When we enjoy the total spaciousness of everything that is, there already is pure pleasure, and we don't necessarily need to look for love or pleasure in sexual contact. The total connection that has never been disconnected is already present.

Whether we are practicing celibacy and solitude or whether we are engaging with another person in a sexual way, sexual desire is not something that is other than what is totally pure. Whether it is an actual movement of sexual desire in the body or the thoughts and emotions associated with that sexual desire, it is all completely pure in its essence.

If we have this unclouded connection with our true sexual nature, then when we are sexually active, everything about that sexual activity—the seeing, tasting, touching, hearing, smelling—we know to be primordially pure and imbued with open intelligence. To enjoy the free-form play of total purity, clarity, total pleasure and complete love without needing to change anything is quite extraordinary.

SEXUALITY IN YOUNG PEOPLE

When young people move into their teenage years and sexual feelings come alive in them, most are told to avoid those feelings. They are told to not explore those sexual feelings with themselves and be self-sexual, and they are cautioned about exploring these sexual feelings with others.

This tremendous energy that appears in young people, which is usually described as sexual energy, is in fact the force in a person to connect with all things and all people. Young people begin to experience this tremendous energy of connection with others at this time of their lives when they also begin to look beyond the confines of the family. But if this energy of connection is made into a belief system and described in erroneous ways, then it becomes an area in which the young person feels limited and confused, and they never really know what to do about this powerful energy.

All over the world we are seeing increasingly sexualized teenagers—or even younger people—who have no understanding of their true sexual nature. We as adults are participating in actions that point young people towards these overly sexualized behaviors, and we are not demonstrating the sort of clarity that would help them in dealing with their sexual urges.

With the role models that young people have in their own families, with friends, television, films, advertising or the celebrities they are often so fascinated with, the examples are often very poor. Today young people are encouraged to enter into an over-sexualized identity, and there's incredible emphasis placed on sexual interaction with no understanding at all of what the sexual energy means.

There is a lot of talk today about freedom of sexual activity, and this is being promoted very overtly and publicly in many forums. For example, the Internet is an example of the very open display of a wide range of sexual activity. Things that were formerly not spoken about or were completely hidden are no longer hidden away in the fantasies of a few people. Anyone who wants to do so can find any expression of sexuality on the Internet, and young people are very readily exposed to these things.

We really have to ask ourselves what kind of freedom we want for ourselves and for our young people. Do we want this kind of freedom that gives license to any sort of expression no matter how harmful it might be, or do we really want to gain confidence in a more fundamental freedom that has a practical application in each one of our own lives and in the lives of people everywhere? This fundamental freedom is not a matter of merely doing whatever one wants to do anytime one wants to do it. It is the freedom that naturally occurs when one lives as the open intelligence of one's fundamental nature.

REAL SATISFACTION

The pattern of sexual desire is very easy to trace: you see an attractive person and you start having all kinds of sensations in your body. You like the way these sensations feel compared to other sensations—like a headache or a sore knee—so you decide, perhaps unconsciously, that you are going to set up more situations where you can have these pleasant feelings.

Once you see that special someone you're attracted to and who will provide more of those pleasant feelings, one of your main missions is to have that special someone be attracted to you. You want to make the desired person see you the way that you want to be seen so that they will be attracted to you. You think, "Aha! This is what he or she really likes, so I am going to mould my behavior to match that, and then they're going to really like me, and I'll get the good feelings I'm looking for."

Does any of this sound familiar? When we look at it this way it really seems rather comical, but when we are lost in all the thoughts, we can feel powerless and overwhelmed. What is for sure is that this is not a sound basis for an honest relationship. This sort of behavior is something you want to confront head-on with the power of open intelligence, and certainly there are more and more people who are gaining certainty in open intelligence who are committed to having honest relationships.

Anything you want out of sexual desire, romantic relationships, intimacy or connection with another human being is going to come from gaining certainty in open intelligence. From certainty in open intelligence and from the vantage of that incredible perspective, you're going to find the satisfaction you are really looking for. You're not going to find it in the same old routines of identification of a target and then seduction of that target by pretending to be somebody you are not. The choice to be clear, honest and open is what we call the path of no bullshit. You really have to get real with yourself and with what you've been up to. But when you do, it can be truly incredible.

TRAINING IN PERVASIVE OPEN INTELLIGENCE

When you take sex to be a special thing that can somehow solve your problems or make you feel better, then it's nothing more than an antidote. It is the same with any other antidote, whether it's money, food, work, relationships, having fun, being entertained or whatever it might be—they can all be employed to make you feel better for a time.

Extreme sexual states and longings can appear, but even amidst those strong sexual feelings you can still experience timeless freedom. It is crucial that you recognize this, because you will face times when this unsatisfied longing will appear, even if you don't feel it now. To train in the timeless freedom of open intelligence guarantees that when these unexpected states come up, you're going to be okay.

At every turn there might be some kind of seductive point of view—money, fame, desire, sex—that we could get involved in that we think is going to make us happy. But no matter how seductive it might be, there really isn't anything there. When we rely on the open intelligence that is the basis of all these seductive influences, then we can really come to know ourselves to be beyond seduction.

What is more important, to get lost in yet another alluring stream of data or to gain familiarity and certainty in open intelligence? What could be better than feeling absolutely okay no matter what comes up? Training ourselves in pervasive open intelligence guarantees that we don't have to run after antidotes in any situation.

INTIMATE RELATIONSHIPS

CHAPTER FIFTEEN

PERFECT RELATIONSHIP

How many of us have gotten together in a relationship and tried to work out all the details of how we are going to live together happily? Each person lays out the structure of their data and negotiates their demands in hopes of clarifying the relationship, but what does that actually bring about? This type of negotiation doesn't lead to complete well-being; instead, it merely leads to more arrangement of data.

Many people are yearning for complete well-being in an ideal relationship, but they are yearning for something that no person or relationship can provide. I've never met a single person who has said, "My partner has made me absolutely happy." Even if someone did say that, it would be misleading, because complete happiness cannot come from another person. If we begin to rely on open intelligence, we will be released from the melodrama that naturally comes with the yearning to get something from a relationship, and only when there is complete release from that melodrama is it possible to have a truly intimate relationship.

From the beginning of our life we want to belong and be understood, we want to love and be loved; however, that often isn't the lived experience many of us actually have. Even though we have this deep longing to be understood, to belong and to be needed, we so often feel that we haven't yet found it.

Maybe we have found the person that we feel we are meant to be with; they are the perfect partner—one who is loving, considerate and understanding, and there is a very strong connection with them. Yet many of the same feelings we've always had in past relationships may still be present—fear of abandonment, fear of loss of love, fear of not being good enough, fear of not being young enough or pretty enough or whatever it might be. Many of us bounce around between all these thoughts and emotions in each relationship we have had in life leading up to the present relationship.

To be able to see into how we have troubled ourselves with all our ideas about things is very important. The love we are looking for is in ourselves. If we find that love, none of the stories we've had about ourselves or anyone else will matter anymore.

When we are able to be happy anywhere, there is no longer a need for a person, place or thing to deliver something that can never be delivered by a person, place or thing. From that perspective, all relationships whatsoever are a place of total joy, but that joy is not rooted in the person, place or thing that is being related to; it is rooted in open intelligence.

By the power of instinctive recognition we reach a place where we feel that we could be married to anyone! That's when we're really ready to get married. When we are able to glide along easily with anyone and everyone in each circumstance that arises, that's when we're really ready to be in a truly intimate relationship.

INTIMACY AS A COUPLE

If two people choose to come together in an intimate relationship, ideally both people would be committed to open intelligence. That commitment to open intelligence really is the best foundation for coming together. Any other context for relationship pales in comparison to this one. If you are in an intimate relationship with someone and it is only you who is committed to getting to know yourself as you really are—and you don't want to leave the relationship—that is perfectly fine.

You can be happy as you are, regardless of what is going on with the other person.

In order for two people to have intimacy as a couple, first in themselves they have to be at ease with everything that appears. With every feeling they have about the people in their lives—the love, the hate, the ambivalence, bad memories, good memories, the hopes, the fears, the realization that they never got what they wanted out of the relationship—they have to let it be *as it is* while they maintain open intelligence. Letting everything be *as it is* is quite different from resisting thoughts, trying to change the thoughts or acting impulsively based on the thoughts.

No matter who you are and no matter what kind of relationships you have, you are going to have to face your data. You could live completely by yourself in a cave for years, and all your data would still be there. Whether you are living in a cave or you are out in the world of relationship, your data are still going to come up. Know that wherever you are, there you are. Wherever you are, that's where all your data will be.

Intimacy doesn't come about by sharing data; it comes about through the profundity of realizing one's own nature. When we recognize this, then we no longer need to look to other people to fill our needs. We know we can look to ourselves, which means that we can look to our true nature.

By the profundity of the practice of short moments of open intelligence, repeated many times we enter into a realm of genuine intimacy with ourselves and with others, to the point that no one is a stranger to us. We live our lives in a joyful way, no matter what's going on. It doesn't mean that we run around giddy with delight; it means that we have found the deep and abiding joy of our own open intelligence, whatever our outer experience may be. We know that no matter what happens in our lives, we will be okay.

RELATIONSHIP WITHOUT EXPECTATION

We may have lived a life where we tended to get wrap
ideas about how we wanted things to be. A very common
scenario is that we look for a special someone who's going to
agree with all of our data, and we think that when we find that
special someone, we will have found true love at last. But then
when we actually find that special someone, we discover that
things are not as we had expected. We ping-pong between
accepting the other person and pushing them away, and we
don't find the pervasive equanimity that is possible in a
relationship.

Entering into an intimate relationship with someone is
something to be extremely watchful about, especially because
each of the partners is going to be committing so much of
themselves to the relationship. It's very helpful to get
completely acquainted with our own nature—and then decide
from there what we want to do about getting together with
someone.

If we do choose to have a relationship with someone, we
don't need to seek anything in the relationship for ourselves; we
know that ultimately there is nothing about getting together with
another person that can either enhance us or take us down. This
is a very, very powerful realization. What is really important to
us is to have complete well-being—whether we are in a
relationship or not—and this is within our grasp in each short
moment of open intelligence.

By the power of short moments we come to know what real
love is. Real love does not come about through making a person
be a certain way. We don't need to have ideas about any
person—either positive or negative. When we start to feel that
we are united with everyone, that's when we really have the
power to be in true intimate relationship with another person.

my seeing that Pete can't set a safe stage for me to show up tenderly.

We find that the love we've been looking for in someone else *have*
is really within us—it's never been anywhere else. We could *to*
seek for it forever in other people, places or things, but we'd
never find it there. Real love is within our own peaceful nature. *brave*

9-25-12 *He does take _____ that*
opening.

CLARITY IN CHALLENGING RELATIONSHIPS

Every situation, no matter what it is, is a training ground for
gaining clarity and insight into all aspects of your life, and the
situations you're in that irritate you the most can be the best
training ground of all. Whatever another person is doing is a
perfect opportunity for you to gain certainty in open intelligence,
and extremely negative situations are where the greatest fruits of
open intelligence are born. They really are—the nastier the
situation, the better.

When you're in a difficult relationship with people with
whom you are linked due to decisions you've made in the past,
then it's really important to recognize that you're not a victim of
the data associated with the situation. If the person should do
things like launching into threatening behavior, trying to
manipulate you or overpower you to get what they want, this is
just the way it is, and there is only so much you can do about
that.

There are always going to be situations where people push
your buttons, and there is often a retribution process that goes
on within us that involves blaming them, making them wrong
and showing what a bad person they are. However, that way of
going about things is really very damaging to your well-being.
By allowing yourself to get hooked into these negative
dynamics again and again, you drown yourself in these data. It
is a no-win situation and it feels totally unpleasant.

In the moment that negative thoughts and emotions about a
difficult relationship come up, it is important to completely rely
on open intelligence without any need to change the thoughts

and emotions in any way. You do not need to repress the thoughts and emotions; you simply remain grounded in open intelligence rather than in the data that are appearing. If you hold to open intelligence, then you can see that the thoughts and emotions about the person emerge again and again, and then they simultaneously resolve.

If you aren't able to be clear and you are pulled along by the thoughts and emotions, then you'll be off on a trip about the situation, and that won't do you any good. The only way to not be ruled by the negative thoughts and emotions is by relying on open intelligence. That's where your power is; it isn't anywhere else.

Most all of us are in relationship with someone else in one way or another, so it's important to gain confidence in our greatest strength so that we can best interact in a peaceful way with other people. This is where the rubber meets the road, so to speak: it's in standing firm in what is ultimately true. No one likes to be in situations with extremely negative people, but there are all kinds of ways to live with that sort of situation if it is a part of our lives.

We cannot force another person to change their behavior. The willingness to change has to come from within them. For example, we could put someone in prison or otherwise try to alter their behavior, but that would not stop the underlying motivation of someone who is out of control. They need to want to see reality for themselves—in whatever way that may come about.

While it is sometimes very difficult to be with a person you are having problems with, you certainly can change your perspective regarding that person. In this regard you really have to come to your own rescue. There isn't anyone else who's going to come to your rescue.

From wide-open clarity you have many more options in dealing with the situation. By securing yourself in open intelligence and allowing everything to be in your face, so to speak, with no need to act impulsively or compulsively, then you become clearer and clearer about what will lead to the best solution. Whatever measures you need to take, you'll see them from open intelligence.

NOT RELYING ON OUR LOVED ONES FOR WELL-BEING

Many of us have harbored the hope that someday we will achieve the perfect relationship with our loved ones. We may have been looking for that, but even if we were able to find it, we would not be able to totally count on it for our well-being. Not only can we not rely on any of our loved ones for complete well-being, we know that at some point either they will leave us or we will leave them. Even if we have a totally deep connection with a person, there is no guarantee that that person is going to be around forever. Either one of us could drop dead in the next minute without warning.

Enjoy everything that is available and at the same time understand its true nature. Know that all of these things that we scamper after—whether it is having the ideal relationship with our loved ones or whether it is in food, money, sex, work, friendships, intimate relationships, having children, pursuing leisure activities, vacations or sports—none of these things can give us complete well-being.

It is not necessary to run around trying to ensure our own well-being and everyone else's well-being, because it can only come from within each one of us. If we are running after all kinds of things, there will be some point where we are exhausted with the running and we will want to just rest.

UNCONDITIONAL LOVE

Many people believe the best way to have a good relationship with another person is through talking about emotional states. This is a very popular idea, but it is really nonsense. If you are constantly talking about your emotional states with other people and they are doing the same with you, that is definitely not the best basis for a relationship.

Instinctive recognition of open intelligence as the fundamental condition of all emotions is the optimal foundation for any relationship. Root yourself there and you will have an easy go of it. If you need to communicate something about emotions, you can do so, but the conversation will no longer be about the emotions alone.

Have you ever been able to get totally clear and connected with anyone through talking about your emotions? Maybe for a brief time it might work and you could feel more connected, but there will always be more emotions to talk about and more things to get clear on. This is an awkward and bumbling way to relate.

There's very little that needs to be talked about in the emotional domain, because the emotions are only temporary appearances. We don't have to get clear about a lot of different emotional states in order to find love, but if we never realize that, we will be blabbering about our emotional states all our lives.

We could sit around and tell endless stories to each other about this, that and the other thing. For example, one person might say, "I feel hurt when you look at me that way," and the other might respond, "Well, I don't mean to look at you that way, but when I was growing up no one listened to me and as a result I have a permanent frown." We may think that by sharing stories like this we have somehow come closer to one another and that this sort of relating is the same as intimacy, but it's not.

This is not to say that by identifying with open intelligence we become robotic and do not have any emotions. Rather, all the emotions that arise are seen in a radically different way. No thought, emotion or experience need obscure the crystal clear love that shines through all appearances.

Love is the naturally occurring perfection of reality *as it is* right here and now. In order to really know what love is, we have to gain certainty in open intelligence to the degree that, no matter what data are appearing, we see them as an appearance of that love. The appearances are not anything to shuffle away, be drawn into or be indifferent about. They are just the pure presence of perfect love.

Once we find this love, we are no longer fixed on changing one another's data or needing to understand our emotional states. We no longer have childish expectations that our romantic partners, friends or family need to fulfill for us. It's so entirely freeing to gain certainty in open intelligence, because we are able to discover the unconditional love that expresses itself without expectation of return love.

TRUE RELATIONSHIP

Sometimes we feel that we need to get into a romantic relationship, because if we do so we will finally have someone to listen to our data. But this isn't what a relationship should be about. We sometimes approach relationships not even knowing that the urge to have a relationship might have come from that disposition of needing someone to listen to our data.

We're meant to enjoy each other and enjoy life together and to take care of each other. This is what true relationship is: to bring greater enjoyment to one another, not less enjoyment. By relying on open intelligence, we see people as they are through seeing ourselves as we are. When we see ourselves as we are and we're able to see other people as they are, then we no *yes!*

longer see them as an object that is somehow going to satisfy our needs. We're together with them in an easygoing way, and we are able to be with people in a way that doesn't involve calamity, hysteria and drama. This is very, very powerful.

THE NATURAL STATE OF LOVE

A lot of times we look for love by trying to arrange a lot of what we take to be loving appearances. We don't really know about love if we only have a description about what love might be. We'll never really know what love is unless we are familiar with our own inner clarity.

So often we hope that another person will love us, but fear that they won't. This subtle point of view informs our actions. Our activity may become contrived because it is based on trying to do certain actions that we consider to be loving and compassionate. The relationship is therefore based on hope and fear—hoping that love will happen and fearing that it won't, and needing another person to love us in order for us to feel loved. *No,* The data that come from hope and fear are often very common in intimate relationships.

When we first get together with our beloved, everything is fantastic. It feels so good; we know there will be nothing like this ever again. We feel like we are the luckiest person on earth. We just want to be together all the time, and there is an openness filled with loving sweetness. But after a while that can begin to change.

There are very subtle data based on cause and effect that come up—the "effect" is the profound love we feel and the "cause" of that profound love is the person we've met. If we think they are the source of the love, then if the love disappears we will think that they are the cause of the disappearance.

at initial feeling of intense love has diminished, we [his] has something to do with the other person. We [for] instance, "Well, I think you need to change so that the love can return. If you stop talking to me the way you do or if you would just remember to put the toilet seat down, then the love would return." We all know what this is like, because we've been through it. When we see this type of situation in such a clear way it seems humorous, but when we're lost in it, it's not humorous at all.

When we start to gain familiarity with open intelligence, our relationships with people change. Our relationships are based in the natural responsiveness and natural compassion of open intelligence, and all our relating becomes unconditional. We find in a very natural way that the relationships that we've had don't look the way they once looked. For example, we may have had a lot of psychological labeling with our partner or in our family about who did what to whom and how we ended up being how we are because of what they did, but through open intelligence we can see this for the nonsense that it is. *not honest to say that.*

very mental *judgment*

When we gain familiarity with open intelligence, we move beyond all of the nonsense and we start to see our partner and our family in a new way. "Wow, what do you know—they're just like me. All the data streams are just whatever they are." Maybe before we needed something from them, but now we know that we don't need anything from anyone. We have tremendous compassion and connection that we may never have had before. *advanced. C'mon now. How about progress?*

really?

This is true in all relationships, whether they're family relationships, intimate relationships or just ordinary encounters with people walking down the street. However, that doesn't mean that we're foolish; it means that our actions flow with total clarity. Some situations we go into, others we don't, and this happens in an effortless way. We are not locked into fixed ideas about things. No matter what happens, we rely on open intelligence, and then we know what to do. When all data are outshone, we have mastery over the illusion of data.

This is a worthwhile life. Until then, life is fraught with uncertainty because of the perceived need to keep different relationships and certain ways of being in place in order to feel comfortable and safe. It's only when comfort and safety are thrown completely out the window and it all goes pell-mell that everything is seen as timelessly free.

CHILDREN AND PARENTING

CHAPTER SIXTEEN

A PARENT'S OWN EXAMPLE

If you are parent, you certainly feel a great responsibility to take proper care of your children, and you want to do what is best for them according to what you have discovered for yourself. You may have become very interested in relying on open intelligence in your own life, but you don't know if your children are ever going to be interested in the same way you are.

What you can do for them is to allow them to see that they have a clear option in their lives: a conventional way of living life which involves focusing on data, or a life of relying on open intelligence. You can describe to them how things shifted for you once you began relying on open intelligence and how what was difficult for you before isn't difficult for you any longer, and you can explain to them how what you have discovered has made a difference in your life. They will, however, have to explore what you have said for themselves and eventually make their own choices.

But even if you never explain anything, a child can sense what is true, because truth is so clear and instinctive. A parent can do a great deal to make sure that the ground is laid for their child, and that comes mostly through the parent's own example. You don't have to preach to your children; they can see the way that you live your life. They see the way you are in relation to your own data and the way you are in relation to their data. "Monkey see, monkey do!" What the little monkeys see the big monkeys doing is what they will tend to do themselves!

Even if your family members or your partners or your kids have no idea what you're up to and don't get it at all, just by your presence you can have an influence on them that they may not even recognize. You can make the lives of everyone you are connected with better, even though they may not know that it is your presence that has done so.

MAINTAINING YOUR OWN HAPPINESS

What should you do when your mommy gets grumpy? A little girl asked this question, but everyone who has a mommy has had to deal with that at one time or another. First of all, if she gets grumpy and then you react against that grumpiness, then you'll both be in a bad mood, won't you? But if you just take a moment to pause and relax without imagining or doing anything, then you can know better what should happen. Maybe you could say to her something like, "We have better conversations with each other when we are friendly than when we are grumpy." So, in this way it's easy, because it fosters friendship, whether it's with your mother or with another person.

We probably all have thought about our mommies, "Oh, why do you treat me like you do!" It might even go so far that we might say, "I wish I had another mommy." Do you ever have thoughts like that? Everyone who has ever had a mommy has had that thought, so you see, that's very normal.

What's important is that you be happy yourself and help make other people happy. Now, if your mommy is grumpy, you can look to being happy yourself, and from that happiness you see what you could do that would be of benefit to her when she is not feeling so well. If she likes coffee, maybe you could get her a cup of coffee, or if she likes to have her back rubbed or to go for walks to the library, you can do those things with her. In the natural flow of things almost everyone gets grumpy, and it's nice to see what we can do to be loving, kind and compassionate with people when they don't feel well.

Sometimes people who are grumpy or who have bad moods are that way a lot of the time, or maybe they are that way most all the time. They may also be unpredictable: half of the time they are grumpy or have some bad mood going on, and then the other half of the time they are pleasant to be with. Whatever it may be, you can always know what to do in any of these situations by maintaining your own happiness. Then you can see how you can best live your life so that it will create happiness for others as well.

WHEN LOVE IS FULLY ALIVE

There are data that can be very, very painful for us. For example, wanting something desperately can be a very painful data stream. This might take the form of wanting success in life or wanting to have a child and also seeing these things as something essential to our long term happiness.

Often we get involved in compulsive seeking for relief and well-being through the attainment of different life experiences. We think falling in love will give us well-being. "Well, that's it. I'm going to get into a relationship, and it will really be great." Then we get into the relationship, and at first everything is glorious. We are totally in love; it feels so good and everything is so ideal. Now that we're in love, we like everyone, even people we didn't like before! We know for sure that we are always going to feel this love.

Almost everyone who falls in love feels this, but it's exceedingly rare that this love lasts. It is rare because it takes exceeding maturity and wholeness for that love to be kept alive. It's only when that love is fully alive in and of itself that it can stay alive in a relationship. An ideal relationship would be where this maturity is fully alive in both people and the relationship is one without expectations.

But if that maturity is not there, then when the love starts to not be present and this falling-in-love love disappears, then we blame the other person for it. Even if we don't do it consciously, we still may blame the other person. We're sure that the other person needs to change in order for this love to come back. This is just the way it goes over and over again. This illustrates the compulsive influence of data.

The falling-in-love love isn't there anymore, and we want it back so desperately. We then think, "Aha! A child is the answer! Let's have a child together." So, the child comes, and at first it's that falling-in-love feeling again, but then the demands of parenting and raising a child set in. It quickly becomes very obvious that there are all kinds of data associated with raising a child. Children are whoever they are, and many of them are not open to reason for a long time. Now, not only are there two adults, but there is a child who may not be open to reason. In fact, they may never be open to reason as long as we know them!

Ideally when we fall in love, we want someone who is a perfect match for us, and when we have a child we want a child who is a perfect match for us as well. We hope that the child will be our tried and true companion throughout life. Well, have we been tried and true companions to our parents throughout life? Even though we seek relationships—whether it's with a significant other or with a child—we haven't really examined what is necessary for true happiness in a relationship.

To have a child does not in itself lead to happiness. Having and raising children, like any other experience in life, is filled with all kinds of data. Once we have a child, not only do we have our own data to deal with, but now we also have the *child's* data to deal with.

What we really need to rely on is what is most essential to our long term happiness, which is gaining certainty in open intelligence. That is more important than anything—more important than any money we can earn, any job we have, any education we get or any child we might have.

THE ULTIMATE MOTHERING

When we truly empower a person by showing them their true nature, one could say that this is the ultimate mothering one could give to another! Mothering is different from caretaking. Often we confuse mothering or parenting with caretaking. To merely caretake a child is different than empowering a child. To empower children is to allow them to see what their strengths, gifts and talents are and how those talents can be of benefit to all. What happens much of the time is that parents do things for the children that the children could have done themselves, but the kids will not learn what their strengths, gifts and talents are if the parents are doing everything for them.

For example, by the time a child is seven years old, they should be able to get themselves up on time for school, make their own lunch and otherwise take care of a lot of the things that parents often do for them—if the children are empowered to do so. It might be considered weird if a child is empowered by a parent in this way at such an early age; however, a child of seven is perfectly capable of taking care of many more things than we expect—if we just allow them to do so. If they are not empowered to make decisions from early on, then that capacity may not become clear in their lives until much later. To support a child in this way is the ultimate parenting. The parent does not need to be an authority that somehow has the answer for everything and everybody.

We have within us a naturally occurring impulse to be of benefit to everyone, but it is not enough to want to be of benefit to everyone; it is important to know *how* to be of benefit to everyone. That's where the true skillful means of a parent come in.

If you are all wrapped up in life and you have a million things going on with many commitments and obligations, that's just the way it is. If you are a parent who is in a difficult relationship with a spouse or partner, and you leave that scene and look for another one, then you will be leaving one scene with its data for another scene which has its own data. If you leave the difficult scene for another one that you think will be easier, you will have to deal with all the guilt and remorse that come from bailing out on the family and children to whom you had made a commitment.

The difficult data you're having don't necessarily get better by taking yourself and all your data with you to another place. The people you've left are wondering where you went and why you went there. Even though it may be tempting to walk out on a troubling situation, it is a move which has consequences. At the same time, I am not in any way suggesting that anyone should continue to stay in an abusive relationship.

Let's say for instance that you've had a very difficult family circumstance, and maybe you have given some consideration to leaving, but at some point maybe you got interested in short moments many times. You want to bring that message to your family, but you don't know how that might work. If you are in such a situation, my suggestion is to continue taking short moments, and you will be amazed at the truly miraculous influence this can have on any situation you are in.

Maybe your partner isn't interested at all in short moments, or they even see it as a threat. Maybe you're trying to encourage your children to rely on open intelligence and they're saying, "I don't want to hear about this anymore!" Yet, you might find after some time that, without doing anything specific, this restful disposition of being you have taken on will somehow have permeated the household. You go about your life relying on open intelligence, and as you do so, your relationships will be such that people will see changes in you. They will appreciate those changes, and maybe they will start relying on open intelligence, too. You may find that they are adopting an easier way to live in a natural way without your having to evangelize at all.

BEFORE HAVING A CHILD

It's so important to be totally clear about one's motives before actually having a child. If you haven't had children yet, it's really important to gain certainty in open intelligence before you decide to have a child, because very often we have children for the wrong reasons. The feeling may come up, "Oh, a baby would be nice. We'll be a family together, and the children will grow up happily, and then they'll go off and build their own lives. They'll start their own families and invite me into their new lives and love me and take care of me when I get old."

You need to have a reality check, because when you bring another human life into the world, it is such a huge responsibility. Some children are naturally predisposed to open intelligence, but they are very, very few, and many others are not naturally predisposed at all. No matter which decision you make regarding having a child, the decision is going to be much clearer if it comes from certainty in open intelligence. You're going to have a much better idea about what you want to do and why you want to do it. You won't have any foolhardy motives for doing what you do.

Being the parent to a child is a lifelong relationship that involves all kinds of things; you never know which way it is going to go. If you are one of those people who has been dreaming of your kids growing up and then taking care of you, that may happen or it may not. Are you taking care of your own parents in the way that you would want to be treated when you are old?

It's really important to bring the ideas about having children out of fantasy and into reality. Some schools use the approach of teaching parenting skills by having the students carry around a ten-pound bag of flour everywhere they go for weeks at a time, as if it were a baby. If they go out on a date, they have to carry that bag of flour or have somebody watch it for them. This doesn't exactly get the sense of having a real baby, but it is good way of getting the students to see the level of responsibility that is involved.

It's also very good to be clear about the kind of world a child would be coming into. Right now we are on the precipice of huge changes, and we are not sure what will happen during the lifetime of a child that we bring into the world. All these are very important considerations before committing to the responsibility of having a child. Gain certainty in open intelligence, and then give birth to future knowledge bearers of pure open intelligence, if you so choose. This is the way to go about it.

THE ULTIMATE OFFERING FOR A CHILD

With a child, just like with yourself, there are all kinds of approaches that can be taken if someone is lost in data. What you want for your child is what you would want for yourself in a situation like that: that they should ground themselves in open intelligence rather than in indulging, avoiding or replacing data. Any child can learn to gain certainty in open intelligence, and as a parent, this is the ultimate offering you can give your child.

Some children are more restful than others and are naturally relaxed and open, and other children are at the other extreme. They're completely out of control, and they may not only cry and scream, they may also hit, kick, bite and do other impulsive things, because they don't know that they shouldn't be doing these things. These days there are more and more children in the world who act in this impulsive manner.

To give your child the opportunity to rely on open intelligence and to continually reinforce this in them is absolutely essential. But let's say that you missed out on the opportunity to do this for your children when they were young. You never had an introduction to relying on open intelligence when the children were small, and you were not able to raise them from that vantage. Now you look back and you regret that you never gave that to your child. Well, you can't go back in time and change things that are already done. You need to rely on open intelligence in the direct encounter with this persistent regret you may have about this issue.

Whether your children are young or they're adults, they have an opportunity to gain certainty in open intelligence. In the same way that you have an opportunity to gain certainty in open intelligence in your own life, your children of whatever age have that same opportunity. It's up to them; in whichever circumstances your children may be, it's truly up to them.

If you do have young children now and they refuse to use open intelligence as a tool in their lives, then that will just be the way it is. Having a child that will not follow your directions is a part of what you have to deal with when you have children. Even though you may think, "I'm going to mold this child into my image, likeness and ideals," that may never happen. There will always be something going on with them that is outside of your picture of the way it is supposed to be.

Whether you're dealing with children or other people you love, when you gain certainty in open intelligence, you immediately see how beneficial that confidence will be to everyone.

If we are lost in the world of point of view, we live in a state of constant disappointment, whether we are conscious of that or not—constantly looking for emotional or intellectual states that are going to be a fixed reference point that we can count on. Because this fixed reference point doesn't exist and can never be found, we're in a state of constant disappointment. We want our friends, family or our loved ones to provide us some kind of satisfaction or fulfillment, and we very much want it from our children as well. We're often disappointed by them, because they don't give us what we have sought from them.

There's only one form of true intimacy, and that's the intimacy that comes from the basic state. That kind of intimacy is totally lucid. It doesn't need anyone to be anything, so it's automatically intimate with everything. When we allow everything to rest in that basic state, then we're automatically intimate with everyone and everything, without trying to be. We're able to go beyond emotional pandering and allow everything to be *as it is*. If we can allow that to be true for ourselves, we can allow that to be true for our children as well.

When we are looking at ourselves as our data, then we are also looking at everyone else as their data. Very often we want to change the data our children have into our data, but this never leads to real well-being, and no manipulation of data can ever give a child permanent well-being. The only place children can ever find permanent well-being is within themselves.

The signs of self-arising wisdom that are demonstrated in clarity, insight, complete mental and emotional stability, compassion and skillful activities are all present in everyone. If we rely on our peaceful nature for short moments many times, swiftly and surely we will find something about ourselves that we never dreamt present. Like a wonderful child who is filled with incredible gifts, strengths and talents, so too every single human being on the face of the earth has the powers of open intelligence already present in them; all we need to do is to access them.

The secret instruction, the golden key, is to be found in short moments, repeated many times until it becomes continuous.

Section Five
Open Intelligence Pervaded by Peace

COMPASSION AND BENEFIT

CHAPTER SEVENTEEN

SEEING YOURSELF EXACTLY AS YOU ARE

Some of the greatest teachers of wisdom who have ever lived have said, "Afflictive states raged in me my entire life." That's a great teaching. There can be all kinds of hardships going on in the life of someone who is wise and aware; however, they have a presence of abiding joy, love and compassion because they aren't split off into self-centeredness and dismay. This is how natural compassion comes about.

By seeing yourself exactly as you are, you become compassionate with yourself, and that compassion for oneself is the source of compassion for everyone. It is possible to cultivate some kind of compassion, but that isn't the same thing as naturally occurring compassion. Splitting off from what is being thought and felt in an attempt to become compassionate leads only to a contrived compassion.

Naturally occurring compassion on the other hand is grounded in not needing to change afflictive states. Even if your thoughts are crazy and all over the place, you can laugh at yourself as you naturally, completely, irrevocably and absolutely rely on open intelligence. That is also where tremendous energy is to be found. In letting yourself be totally naked, exactly as you are, you find a tremendous resource of energy, intelligence and caring.

Humility, openness and willingness come about from allowing yourself to be as you are. An afflictive state may appear, and you see that open intelligence is appearing along with it and is inseparable from it. You know that you're gaining certainty in open intelligence through the display of open intelligence associated with that recognition. This is how you gradually and instinctively recognize the indivisibility of everything and you come to have true compassion for all.

UNCONTRIVED COMPASSION

Compassion is ever present for a person who abides in their identity as open intelligence. That compassion doesn't look like any one thing, and it doesn't look like most of the ideas about what compassion should be. Many people believe that compassion is a nicey-nice state or only having positive thoughts and emotions, but that's not true compassion. True compassion is naturally present and naturally free *as it is*.

We come to that understanding by seeing that all of our own thoughts, emotions, sensations and experiences are naturally free. In other words, we know what's going on all the time, and through that it becomes possible to know what to do and how to act in every situation. That's really what compassion is: knowing what to do and how to act in every situation. If we're trying to contrive compassion, it's impossible to see that we're innately compassionate. Our innate compassion can only be recognized by growing certainty in open intelligence. It's not anything that anyone has to try to cultivate.

For example, say you're at the grocery store in a long line. You can't wait to get out of there, and then somebody comes and breaks in line right in front of you. Maybe another person walks up, they see the other person get in line in front of you, so they cut in line too! You're totally exasperated and you're thinking "What's going on with these people?" If you've been cultivating compassion, the tendency might be to say, "Okay, to get upset with these people isn't the correct disposition. I need to be compassionate, so I'll just let them go ahead and I'll try to deal with my anger towards them."

Let's say though that these people break in line in front of you, and you feel an upsurge of resentment, hostility and rage— from something very minimal to something extremely overt. No matter what it is, rely on open intelligence and see what the best response to the situation would be. Don't get into the game of contriving patience and compassion or trying to be a certain way. Compassion is in stable open intelligence; it's not found in trying to be a certain way. This is really important, especially if you've been a do-gooder, and many of us have been do-gooders all of our lives, right?

Compassion already exists within everything, so it doesn't need to be made up. In the same way that the brilliance of a diamond is inherent to the diamond, compassion is inherent in open intelligence.

THE PURPOSE OF LIFE

Whether we know it or not, every single day we are involved with finding the purpose of life. It is an aspiration that is natural to a human being, but most of us are uncertain as to what the purpose of life is. If we don't know the purpose of life and we don't know anyone else who knows, then it may be very difficult to resolve that issue within ourselves.

The purpose of life is very, very simple: to benefit ourselves and to benefit others. By the power of benefiting ourselves, we then have the power to benefit others. The term "benefit" can mean different things to different people. Some people might say, "I'm benefiting myself because I have a good job, make plenty of money, own a house and a car and I maintain my family. I benefit others because I am giving them jobs, and I am nice to people in general." This is benefit of a certain sort, but this is a very limited scope of benefit compared to what we are capable of.

This concern about the purpose of life boils down to the fundamental issue of what we're capable of as human beings. Most of us spend our entire life never knowing what we are capable of, nor do we ever meet anyone who might know what we are capable of.

If we look into the nature of life, we can say that no action can occur without the mind, and nothing can be known without the mind. The mind is key; it is the source of all perceptions. Everything we know about ourselves, the world and others we know through the mind and its fundamental operating system, which is open intelligence. When we understand that the engineered-in purpose of the mind is to benefit ourselves and others, we can really come to ask, "How can I explore this possibility that my mind is actually innately of benefit?"

Most of us never learn that our mind can innately be of benefit. Instead we spend our whole life at war with our mind. We are afraid of ourselves, and we are afraid of many of our thoughts and emotions. We are like a micromanager trying to make our thoughts better thoughts, our emotions better emotions, and our experiences better experiences. We really don't understand that the mind has an innate benefit that is completely beyond trying to figure out what to do about emotions, thoughts and experiences.

The fundamental nature of the mind is a stable expanse that is calm and clear at all times. The calmness and clarity of the mind is present in every single perception. There's never anything that is known without this fundamental stability and open intelligence of the mind present within it.

COMPLETE CONNECTION WITH EVERYONE AND EVERYTHING

As long as you are focused on your own aches and pains—whether they're mental, emotional or physical—you will have a very limited view, and your options will be very restricted.

When your certainty in open intelligence is such that you can naturally and easily rely on open intelligence, then you have complete connection with everyone and everything. You are no longer only concerned with your own body, thoughts, emotions and experiences. You rely completely on open intelligence and are completely sensitive to all of the pain and suffering that are occurring and to the blissful compassion and love that are the foundation of everything.

What is more, when you become clear and lucid within yourself, then you are clear and lucid about everything. When you really see in a profound way what makes you tick, then you immediately see what makes everybody else tick. You know why people do what they do—from the presidents of nations to the person begging in the street, from the great saints to the murderers and maniacs. In a very ordinary, simple, human way you are looking at other people you had always been baffled and befuddled by, and suddenly you see, "Wow, they are overwhelmed with their data just like I used to be."

You realize that you are the dynamic space that is the basis of all that appears. The one hundred percent devotion to open intelligence and the compassion that appears naturally within that devotion open up a life that you could never have conceived of. This kind of compassion can't be cultivated; it's naturally occurring. It's the firsthand instinctive realization of the compassionate nature and intent of everything. This is what guarantees you freedom in all data.

THE UNIVERSALITY OF EXPERIENCE

While some people are very loving, other people aren't, and there are all kinds or people in between. Rather than adopting positions such as, "Oh, everyone is filled with love. Isn't it wonderful!" or "Everyone is so hateful and awful and the world's a terrible place," much better is to have a clear understanding that is free of all extremes. Compassion is allowing yourself to be exactly as you are and others to be exactly as they are, and to be steadfast and unafraid in the direct encounter with each.

Compassion doesn't mean just being nice and having nice thoughts. Real compassion is radical compassion, which is kindness coupled with ferocity. Sometimes kindness is called for, sometimes ferocity is called for. If we only cultivate good thoughts and emotions, then that wouldn't allow for the beneficial compassion that can be ferocious. If we only cultivate good thoughts and emotions, there would be no clearheaded insight into situations that arise and the possible means that are available to deal with the situation.

Within us are already-present love, clarity and energy, which are all synonymous with our own open intelligence, and when we fully rely on open intelligence, tremendous compassion arises naturally in us. We go through a dramatic shift where, instead of all our data being about us and relating back to a personal somebody, we start to recognize that everyone has the sorts of painful thoughts we have.

The next time that you're overwhelmed by afflictive states and you're maybe imagining how bad it can get and all kinds of terrible scenarios, just know that everyone, everywhere has felt that kind of emotion at some point in their lives. Whatever challenging situation you may be facing—whether it's a heart attack, cancer, a severely depressive state or any other kind of human experience—you are sharing that same experience with many, many other people. The experience is not particular to you, no matter how personal it may seem.

THE PRECIOUS OPPORTUNITY OF HUMAN LIFE

The dynamic energy of the vast expanse of open intelligence fills everything completely, and it can be described in many different ways. But whatever it is, it is *as it is*. There's no place to get to, nothing to shy away from, nothing to be afraid of.

When you look at nature, you see that nature is effortlessly beneficial. No matter what happens, everything naturally resolves in space. Even if something cataclysmic happened—a meteor hit planet Earth or nuclear missiles flew back and forth and life as we know it was destroyed—nature remains naturally at ease and ordered in its own way. When we are at ease in our being, we tap into that natural order of everything and we are in harmony with ourselves and with life. We know what it means to be truly human. To be a truly real human being is to be at ease—just like nature is at ease.

Human life is a precious opportunity, and there are two opportunities that are especially precious: to benefit yourself and to benefit others. When you become alert to this precious human opportunity, you naturally want to know how to go about benefiting yourself and others.

This self-benefit and benefit of others is already present within you. It isn't something you get from somewhere else. As everything is a single nondual expanse, where would it come from? Getting in touch with that benefit is very straightforward, simple and uncomplicated; it's not something that you need to strive for decades in order to achieve. In the same way that you wouldn't need to strive to achieve the color of your eyes, you don't need to strive to attain this benefit.

The practical application of benefit is superb helpfulness— the inability to restrain the flow of love in any way. It is the flow of completely unrestrained helpfulness that sees through everything and which never sees anything as other then itself. In seeing through everything, everything is seen to be equal.

When you see how you have fooled yourself all your life by believing all your data, you develop compassion for yourself. When you see what you have put yourself through, you instantaneously have compassion for everyone else, because you know everyone else has been in the same boat. You are no longer in the position of saying, "Oh, my data streams are completely different from yours, and mine are more important."

Everyone has the urge to be of benefit, but unless you discover it for yourself or someone shows you how to bring it into full being within yourself, you spend your life dreaming only very small dreams and settling for just a mere glimpse of your genius.

With anything you have ever dreamt about being or doing, any kind of benefit you want to contribute or anything else you want to contribute to the world, by the sole practice of relying on open intelligence you will see more new ways of being beneficial than anything you had ever dreamt possible. You will tap into that timeless part of yourself that is more ancient than ancient. You will see a way of affecting so many more people than you ever thought possible.

PEACE IN US, PEACE AROUND US

CHAPTER EIGHTEEN

CHANGE IS POSSIBLE

We as a human race haven't been able to get along with each other. Well, this is something so obvious that it might appear that it wouldn't have to be stated, but we have to know where we are in order to get to where we're going. If we want to know where we are, then we have to admit that we haven't been able to get along and that we haven't *known* how to get along. First of all, many of us can't get along with ourselves, and because we can't get along with our own data, it makes it impossible for us to empathize with others in a natural way and to connect with them.

Is it possible that there is something that we don't yet know that we can learn to help us get along? Yes, there is such a thing! It is found in acknowledging our natural perfection for short moments, repeated many times, rather than being lost in all our data. It is the one simple change in the use of the mind that's equally accessible to everyone, which allows us to get along with ourselves as we pass through the stages of life and which allows us to get along with others. This is not a passive form of getting along that limits itself to "you do your thing and I'll do mine," but a way of actually feeling connected to every other being on the face of the Earth and to the planet itself.

What we need to recognize first of all is that unity and peace are important to us and also that change is possible. If we think, "Change can never come about; just look at the situation we're in now," then we'll just demoralize ourselves. But if we say, "Change is possible, and it begins with me," then all of a sudden change becomes very achievable.

We share this planet Earth as well as the basic human needs for water, food, clothing and shelter. We also have the need for health care, education and work that will allow us to contribute our strengths, gifts and talents, and we need time to rest, reflect and play.

We as a human race haven't quite developed the willingness to share resources equally. As it is now, the United States and Europe consume an enormous percentage of the world's resources—a percentage which is way out of balance when compared to the rest of the world. Through the balanced view of open intelligence, we develop the willingness to share equally all the resources that are available to us.

In the balanced view is a natural sense of cooperation, a natural sense of wanting to share equally with others and of wanting to make sure that everyone is provided for and taken care of. It is a natural sensibility that looks around and sees who might need assistance or who might need something that they don't have. The natural response is to want to give to them what they need.

This is another part of the tremendous energy of open intelligence; it holds within it a natural empathy and sympathy and compassion, and these constitute the willingness to share in a very fundamental and equal way.

REAL WORLD PEACE

World peace is possible, but it's only possible in one way, and that is through individual inner peace. It's not going to come about from an external source; it can only come about within individuals, and the simple instruction for bringing that about is short moments of peace, repeated many times, until the short moments become continuous.

Why is this the instruction? Because many of us have no familiarity with the peace within ourselves. For most of us a form of peace becomes evident because we've been cultivating some kind of positive state, but that's not what the practice of short moments of peace is based on. Short moments of peace is based on seeing that everything that appears rests in peace, whether it's a positive, negative or neutral appearance. This is markedly and radically different from avoiding, replacing or indulging appearances or trying to cultivate peaceful states.

The practice of short moments is something that is available to everyone equally. It does not require any intellectual speculation or dogma. It's only a matter of that short moment of peace being repeated again and again. We don't have to keep up the short moments of peace forever, because the short moment becomes longer until it completely dissolves the need to take short moments. At that point the peaceful nature that's always been at the basis of everything becomes evident.

Trying to bring about world peace merely by reforming existing institutions is not the way to go. The only way we can truly reform humankind is by people finding real peace within themselves and demonstrating to others what they have found in their own lives. In this way peace can spread quickly all over the world.

War and many of the other ways that people relate to each other are based on aggression, competition and humiliation, and as long as we feel that these types of approaches are necessary, they will be. We have ended up in a world of conflicting ideologies, where nations war against each other in the name of their god. This way of being is not natural to human beings, and this is why people feel tense and uptight—even terror stricken.

When we make peace with the war within ourselves, then we can see how that can be possible everywhere, but we can't see how it can be possible everywhere without first seeing it within ourselves. These very much go together: peace within ourselves equals peace everywhere.

PEACE ZONE

Human beings are able to bring about peace themselves, but it's not a matter of expecting some authority figure to do the work for us. *We* have to take responsibility. How willing are we to end the war within ourselves? How willing are we to abide in the peaceful part of ourselves that pervades everything? How willing are we to acknowledge that we already have perfect stability in ourselves?

When we begin to gain certainty in open intelligence, what we're really doing is making ourselves into a peace zone. As communities of people that are maintaining open intelligence as their basis come about worldwide, they create very powerful collective peace zones within human society. The importance of gaining certainty in open intelligence cannot be overestimated, because a peace zone—whether individual or collective—is created that is free of hatred, arrogance, fear and envy.

In some ways human society has become less peaceful rather than more peaceful. Terrorism, whether it's physical or psychological, is widespread in human culture, and it's widespread because it's present within individuals. We're all familiar with the movements of hatred that are developing all over the world, but what we need to see is that we ourselves have had all kinds of hateful, arrogant, fearful and envious data. We haven't known what to do with them except to take countermeasures by cultivating good traits. Cultivating niceness and goodness can be comforting to one degree or another, but that has never brought human society into a fully peaceful condition.

We can know that we're taking the most powerful of all political actions by making certain that we are optimal human beings. When we become peace zones within ourselves, we become optimal human beings, and we enter into the optimal condition of humanness. When we call ourselves forth to become a peace zone, we are taking a very, very powerful political action. Through people informing and supporting one another we have the means to bring about peace zones at the grassroots level throughout the world. If we want it, we can have it, but it's up to each one of us individually.

It's so important for each of us to take up short moments of peace repeated many times, because by doing so we fortify ourselves as a peace zone, where hatred, fear, envy and arrogance are absent. You could call a person like this a wisdom warrior! Wisdom warriors create peace zones in themselves and in the world.

It's urgently important to do everything in our power to create peace zones in all aspects of life. Give yourself the greatest opportunity for equanimity in your own life by creating a setting for yourself where it's easy to maintain open intelligence. From there you'll see what it's like to live peacefully and happily.

The more happiness you cultivate within yourself by maintaining open intelligence, the more naturally you'll find yourself surrounded by other people who are doing the same. To form community with other people who are cultivating open intelligence and who are free of hatred, arrogance, envy and fear is a very, very powerful way to live.

RESOLUTION OF HATRED

Not everyone is willing to establish themselves as a peace zone, and that is just the way it is. You simply let other people be as they are, and when they want to come along and join in the effort for peace, they will, but until then there is no use in trying to force them to do so.

If people are angry with you or even hate you, do what you can to make peace with them. If they're acting harshly towards you, invite them to be at peace with you in the most appropriate way you can find. The best basis for resolving a conflict is that each person takes responsibility for their part in creating the conflict.

Sometimes, however, people are hateful to others without any provocation. In that case, the person who initiates the attack is filled with negative feelings, and that is the sole cause of the conflict. You may have had no part in creating the situation, but you can try to help them come to terms with what they're doing, and that is best done through your own unwavering example of peaceful relating. By more and more individuals becoming peace zones and not promoting hate by hating back, more and more impetus will be given to ending this very painful way of living, where people hate themselves and hate others.

The reason we hate other people is because we hate many things about ourselves. It is that simple. However, when we no longer hate ourselves, we will no longer hate others. Hatred is very ingrained in each of us as long as we hate certain thoughts, emotions or experiences we have. If we hate or fear these things about ourselves, we automatically hate and fear them in others, too. We can't withstand that feeling of hatred within ourselves—and we don't know how to resolve it—so we project it outwards towards the government, the president, other political leaders, other races or religions or whatever it might be.

When those things that we hate or fear about ourselves appear and we're tempted to deal with them in some way through a countermeasure or an avoidance, rather than doing that we completely relax, and the emotion will eventually resolve itself. In the resolution of all these hateful and fearful data we'll find an explosion of wisdom that we've never seen before. This is the wisdom of innate peace. Nothing could be more important than educating human beings about this means of becoming a peace zone.

NON-CONFLICTUAL RELATIONSHIPS

To have relationships that are without conflict is definitely something that we want for ourselves and for everyone else. It is truly possible for human society to live this way. However, we first have to see that it's possible to be non-conflictual within ourselves and to see that all appearances appear in an expanse in which there is no conflict.

Once we see that about ourselves, we become capable of being non-confrontational with others. We see that whatever anyone else's responses in life might be, those responses need not push our buttons anymore. Whatever is appearing is just whatever is appearing.

For example, the feeling may come up, "Oh, that person does not understand me at all, so why should I even bother with them?" But it is really excruciating to spend our whole life wanting to be understood and rejecting people because we think they don't understand us.

It's important to see that these stories we have adopted are completely unnecessary. We could spend all of our life wanting to be understood, wanting to be liked or wanting to be respected and looked up to, but this is a very small space to live from.

If people come together who have realized that the nature of all of their experience is non-conflictual, then their relationships will be easeful and open because there is nothing in the way. There is no diving into personal data streams or positions of neediness and expectation. There's just complete openness, compassion and love. In this way, the emphasis in life is no longer one of self-centeredness, but one of benefit for all.

The non-conflictual ground of everything is already entirely beneficial, so the more we abide as that, the more we realize that the ground of our being is beneficial by nature. We don't need to try to be of benefit. It just naturally is that way.

We want to have relationships that are non-conflictual—not just for a day or two now and then—but relationships that for years and years are completely non-conflictual and filled with love, clarity, joy and bliss. Making this evident in the world starts with each one of us.

PEACE BEYOND ALL WAR

When we find within ourselves the utter peace that ends all war, we'll know how to build a human society that doesn't have war. That's the only way; the end of war will never happen on the battlefield or at the negotiation table. We have to develop an entirely new perspective in this matter.

Some of us live in countries where we are forced to participate in war in some way because our country is at war. If we want to continue being a citizen of that country, we may have to make a decision. If we choose to not be part of the warmaking effort of that country, then we'll have to take extraordinary measures that really take us outside the usual realm of choices that most people in the country are making.

Some people live in countries where there aren't such overt wars going on, but even for them things could change at any moment. There could be some kind of extreme political or social upheaval, a terrorist attack could occur or their country could be invaded by another country. We don't know what's going to happen next, and we can't count on any of the things we think we can count on. We can't count on our government, our country or on the current state of affairs.

We have to be radical warriors within ourselves, where we really totally stand up for peace in a way that is clear. We have to stop relying on wishful thinking and fantasy schemes about getting into some kind of idealized state of peace. We have to realize that what we are, we are right now, and only by relying on what we are right now can we realize what we truly are.

This is what is offered in short moments, many times. No matter what the issue is that we are concerned about or involved in, the most powerful solution is going to come from certainty in open intelligence.

OUR INNATELY PEACEFUL NATURE

As much as we as a human race might want world peace, world peace has been beyond our grasp. Instead, what we have today are new forms of war and new ways of dominating and taking power over others, either individually or collectively.

We want to ask ourselves, "How can I make a difference right here, today, in my own life?" We can make a difference by connecting with our own already-present inner peace. Each one of us has a contribution to make: in each short moment of peace that we take, we add a short moment of peace to the storehouse of peace that belongs to everyone in the world. In doing so, we are planting a seed of peace that will grow and flourish.

Peace affirms itself, and when it is acknowledged as a natural potential within each of us, then it becomes obvious. However, world peace becomes obvious only in individuals; it does not become obvious through proclamations about world peace, philosophies about world peace or political statements about world peace. World peace only becomes evident in individual human conduct.

When we rely on short moments of peace, repeated many times, increasingly we have clarity in our thinking as well as mental and emotional stability—rather than fear and confusion. Great insight into our already peaceful nature as well as compassion, empathy and sympathy are naturally present in each short moment of peace. We are introduced to our innate skillfulness to know what to do and how to act in all kinds of situations and circumstances. Where are all these wonderful qualities and characteristics? They are in our already peaceful nature, and not anywhere else. If we don't know that yet, we need to make use of the practical know-how that is available to us in short moments, repeated many times.

Once we identify our peaceful nature, it carries us through every circumstance. Our own peaceful nature is what we can count on, no matter what is going on. We could experience disease, death, hurricanes, earthquakes or war; we don't know when the next challenging occurrence is going to hit close to home. If our well-being is dependent on not having one of these things occur, then when they *do* occur in our lives, we will assume that our well-being will be lost.

What we really need to count on is the well-being that is innate to us. Our innately peaceful nature—unchanging and unruffled—is always feeling well, no matter what is going on. By the power of our peaceful nature we will have leadership of every single moment within each day of our lives, and we will have the leadership at death that only our peaceful nature can provide.

UNFLAPPABLE EQUANIMITY

Most of us have the idea that war and peace are opposites, but war never jumped out of peace to become something other than peace. We've believed that negative states or negative circumstances like war have somehow separated out from peace and well-being, and we think that the negative states are in one place fighting against the well-being that's in another place. But the negative states are in fact inseparable from well-being.

In short moments we come to see that data, whether positive or negative, flow on by within our peaceful nature. They never jump out of our peaceful nature, and they are always nothing but our peaceful nature. It is extremely important to recognize this. The flow of data is to our peaceful nature like space is to space. Just as no part of space is different from another part of space, the flow of data and our peaceful nature are not two different things. Our negative states and our feelings of worthlessness, depression, the bleakest dark days—or our absolute joy, greatest achievements and complete well-being— all come from the same essence. There's nowhere to go! The only well-being there will ever be is right here, right now.

Take it easy, keep it simple, relax and know that by tapping into your own peaceful nature you take a stand for world peace in a demonstrable way that guarantees your own peace at the very least, and there is no greater wealth in life than your own peace.

The unflappable equanimity of our peaceful nature is imbued with the most powerful intelligence, the most powerful diplomatic skills and the most powerful skillful means for taking care of any kind of situation. There can be intense anxiety, intense panic, intense physical pain, but it has never been separated out from total and complete peace. This is what we discover about ourselves.

BE THE CHANGE YOU WANT TO SEE IN THE WORLD

CHAPTER NINETEEN

TRUE CHANGE FROM WITHIN

Where does true change come from? Does it come from political parties or governments? No, political parties and governments are only abstractions. No matter how powerful a political leader is, he or she is incapable of giving inner peace to the people that they are governing. Real change comes from individual people. We have to look within ourselves and say, "What is the change that is needed in me that will bring about the kinds of changes I want to see in the world?"

The change needed is the one simple change each one of us has the power to make: the choice to recognize open intelligence in every moment or not. True change is located in open intelligence. By committing to short moments of open intelligence repeated many times, we tap into our innate peaceful nature and natural perfection.

We will never have peace within ourselves through rearranging external circumstances. Rather than looking to organizations to bring about world peace, we have to create a peace zone within ourselves. World peace will never come about through legal codes or international treaties. It has to come about through finding peace within.

So many of us settle for the status quo, and we don't see any possibility of anything other than that. We have to realize that we have perfection already present within ourselves, but it isn't a destination to be gotten to, and it isn't somewhere off in the future. It's present in each and every thought, emotion, sensation and experience we have.

We need to ask ourselves, "Am I willing to be a hero?" We have to find that which is heroic in us and claim it for ourselves. It is really important to know that we can, dare I say it, save the world. It's up to all of us together to do that. What we really need is the audacity of perfection—perfection which is the complete peace, clarity, compassion and ethical spontaneity that is already present in us in each moment. We have to see that world peace is right here in us.

If that innate inner peace is not recognized, then even if there were complete nuclear disarmament, all armies were disbanded and an abundant life could be created for every single person on earth, individual peace would not be ensured. The people who have abundance in their life and everything they need—has that ensured their inner peace?

By the power of open intelligence, which is the basis of every single perception, we ground ourselves in the perfect peace and spontaneity of each moment. By returning to that again and again, it becomes the basis for our actions in the world. In this way our actions are grounded in natural ethics, profound insights, mental and emotional stability, clarity, laser-like skill and the power to fulfill creative intent in all situations.

THE PERFECT ENVIRONMENT IS WITHIN YOU

There are a lot of big ideas in the world that are very compelling, but if those big ideas come only from the tired conventions of the past, then to continue with them will only be like running around on a hamster wheel chasing one experience after another. There are many ways to come at the numerous environmental issues that we are facing in today's world, but the only way those problems will ever be solved will be by finding the perfect environment that is already within you. If you are interested in environmental action, that is the best environment in which to take action.

If you really want to be an advocate and example of idealism about the environment or any other issue, then you want to find an ultimate kind of idealism that is free from any specific interpretation of idealism. You want to find something so free that it's even free of the focus on the self and all the self's big ideas. Make no mistake about it; finding that freedom is the ultimate action to take. That is what it means to be really radical.

If you're young, you probably have a long life ahead of you, and you want to ground yourself now in what is real, rather than waiting until you are old and gray and too tired to even be interested. But even if you are older, this is the perfect time to ground yourself in your own natural perfection and innate mental and emotional stability. If you ground yourself in what is real, you can have a joyful happy life all the way along, no matter what happens.

You have to see in your own experience that everything is seamlessly unified, and only then can you bring real change into the world. If you are interested in education, politics, the environment, health care, science, technology or any field of inquiry whatsoever—the greatest offering you can ever make to the world you live in is a realization of natural perfection in your own experience.

Why not start there and see where it takes you? Real change is not a matter of modeling the radical change that is so needed today on old, tired ideals that have failed us. Real change will come from resting in the complete non-activity of every single moment. That "non-activity" is what gives you the tremendous energy and insight to bring about radical change in the world.

INCREDIBLE POWER TO BE OF SERVICE

Recently there was an article in the newspaper about a young girl who had epileptic seizures and who had been verbally abused for that reason by other students at several schools she had attended. These students had been horribly cruel to her, called her awful names and had even created a hateful website directed at her. She had been hounded out of each of the schools, and no one had come to her aid.

It so happened that two teenage girls heard about this situation and were very moved by the plight of this young girl. On their own they put together a campaign that resulted in many people writing the girl letters of support. These two teenagers showed through their example that there is a way to not be ruled by passivity and indifference and to come to someone's aid to really help them.

This is the sort of effort one would want to see when injustice comes to light. If, on the other hand, we have the attitude, "I don't want to stand up and say anything, because I don't want to get involved, or maybe I'll get in trouble or be criticized," we are cowering in the corner in the face of injustice.

All these things that are acted out in the world are the unresolved issues that are going on within us. If we hold back, pretend like nothing is happening and refuse to take action, then the pervasive negativity that we see all around us will be allowed to continue to grow.

We have to be willing to say, "I am not going the way of the crass mass, no matter how many people are going that way." We have to be willing to walk away from the negativity, passivity and indifference, and that happens when we are no longer mastered by the data that appear. When we gain certainty in open intelligence, we gain incredible power to be of service to the world in a way that's unimaginable, because we are no longer ruled by the conventional frameworks of point of view.

SUPREME AND SUBLIME ACCOMPLISHMENT

True political change will come from the grassroots level in countries all around the world, and this will become more and more obvious in the generations to come. The idea of divided nations set apart from one another is passé, and the idea of one nation or a few nations being dominant over all others is completely passé. This will fade out in the groundswell of world unity and service that is coming, but this unity and service can only come from individuals impassioned by finding peace within themselves and standing for nothing else but that peace.

It is a radical and revolutionary political action to find inner peace within yourself. The greatest revolution is in claiming personal peace for yourself—and not giving up until you find that. Your undying commitment to that peace automatically benefits everyone else. You don't have to contrive the action of being of benefit to anyone; you are being of benefit to everyone by finding peace within yourself, and there is nothing more powerful than a sincere personal example. You don't have to launch any grand plans in order to be of benefit to everyone. If nothing else should ever come out of your life than this extraordinary inner peace, that in itself will be a supreme and sublime accomplishment.

GREAT ASPIRATION

There is a pandemic of emotional and mental instability in the world that has led to extreme discord among peoples, whether it is discord that we experience in ourselves or discord between nations. The most beneficial way to deal with this instability is to identify with the basic state of open intelligence for short moments, repeated many times. Through this simple practice we tap into our fundamental intelligence, which is naturally of benefit to all.

At some point we need to let go of the focus on personal preoccupations like work, possessions, entertainment and intimate relationships. By recognizing and relying on open intelligence, these things aren't any longer seen as being the way to well-being. When a person is released from the confining individual identifications that come from self-focus, a whole new world opens up.

If you have great aspirations in your life, the power to achieve those aspirations is going to come from introducing yourself to yourself. You want to ground yourself in what you really are before you get into the whirlwind of realizing your personal ambitions. You're not going to have a clear idea of how to do what you want to do until you ground yourself in the true ground, which is your own peaceful nature.

By gaining complete confidence in your natural perfection, you're able to act with a lot of power and insight. If you have aspirations to do something of benefit to the world, you have to strengthen yourself with *true* strength. If you have that true strength, you'll be able to endure all of what's going to be thrown at you, high and low. If you don't ground yourself, then the wonderful things people say about you will sway you, and the devastating things that are said will upset you. You don't want to either be swayed by praise or upset by criticism; you want to follow a steady course towards realizing your highest aspirations.

Clearheadedness, steadiness, profound insight, complete mental and emotional stability, knowing what to do and how to act in every situation—this is what you want as the basis of any kind of aspiration you have to be of benefit to the world.

THE BEST QUALITIES OF LEADERSHIP

When we are aware of our own strengths, gifts and talents and how we can contribute them, then we can also see the gifts, strengths and talents of others and support them in expressing those talents. We can support them, if they want that support, in taking leadership of those gifts within themselves.

When we find within ourselves complete mental and emotional stability, insight, compassion, skillful means and the power to fulfill creative intent, then we know what to look for in a leader. We are able to see the difference between an imposter and a genuine hero. We need to know what we're looking for before we can have it. We should accept only the leaders with complete mental and emotional stability, profound insight, compassion, demonstrable skillful means and the ability to accomplish what will be of benefit to everyone. The heroes and leaders we need are the ones who have these qualities and characteristics, and we should be firm in only accepting these qualities in our leaders. Courage has to be present, and this courage is not something that can be cultivated.

The leaders we need for our struggling world must have inner peace themselves, and they must completely stand up for that alone. They need to be in a position of such peace and attainment of perfection within themselves that their motives are unquestionably sincere and genuine.

We want leaders who *know* us! Of course, by that I don't mean that they know us personally; rather, because they know themselves so completely, they know the human condition, and through that they are able to really know others. A leader with this gift can affect many, many people in a way that a leader who lacks this self-knowledge or who is only interested in personal power cannot.

Open intelligence is the basis of self-leadership, and self-leadership is found in open intelligence. The two are inseparable like the color blue is inseparable from the sky. By the power of recognition of open intelligence and through relying on it for short moments, many times until continuous, we realize that we are the leaders we have been seeking.

THE BEST WAY TO SOLVE PROBLEMS

There are many, many problems in the world, and humankind is in a very frightening state of affairs. Even though we have accomplished tremendous things in terms of science and technology, when it comes down to our own well-being and our ability to have complete mental and emotional stability, we know comparatively little. We're just beginning to understand how these qualities can come about in ourselves.

Without complete stability, it is very difficult to deal with our problems in a skillful way. Unless we have clearsightedness, clarity and lucidity within ourselves, there is no way we can come up with ample solutions to the problems we are facing.

When people get together with other people to form organizations to try to solve problems, it is very difficult to come together and find solutions if they do not feel at ease with themselves. The best way to solve problems is for people to gain certainty in open intelligence, look at the problems clearly and then set about solving them. If the people in the organization are lost in all their data, they may be incredibly brilliant, but they will be trying to proceed in their work without having full ease and open intelligence within themselves. These brilliant people come together in an organization, but they are not clear in themselves, and as a result the solutions they come up with will reflect that lack of open intelligence.

No matter how brilliant the data streams are, the solutions will never be definitively conclusive because they come only from the limitations of reified knowledge. They don't come from our natural intelligence that is beyond learning and which is pulsating with wisdom, compassion and absolute clarity. We have to decide what we want as a human society. It depends on each one of us: what do we want ultimately?

It is important to first recognize open intelligence within ourselves, then we'll be ready to tackle the world. We'll be able to engage in actions that are laser-like, brilliant, incisive and very, very clear; we'll be able to take action in a way that really draws many people together in a very skillful way. We'll be in a unique position, because we will be free from our own data as well as free from the data of everyone else around us. From that place of total strength, we are exceptionally capable, because we can be in any organization in the world without getting wrapped up in personal conflicts.

POWER TO THE PEOPLE

One of the things I noticed when I was politically active in the 1960s was that, even though the supposed motivation was peace and love and power to the people, the people who were talking about these ideals were not peaceful or loving themselves. As long as we couldn't find a way to be peaceful ourselves, there never could be any real power to the people. Real peace and love must be based on the ability of each individual to exhibit peace and love in him or herself; real peace and love will not come merely by demanding it from society.

I learned a lot at that time by watching myself and my peers in the peace movement. I became disillusioned early on with the whole movement, because the peace that was being advocated was not present in the people I worked with, nor was it present in me. In fact I never met a single person in whom it was present. Even if the ideal behind the movement was fantastic, for the most part it was just a lot of rhetoric and inflamed language.

I never gave up on the idealism I had then, but instead of focusing on trying to get corporations, organizations and governments to change, I started focusing on what I could do to bring about substantial change in myself and in other people. I saw that there was a way that the people of the world could be peaceful and loving, and that was what I wanted.

If we look at a term like "power to the people," what this really means is that we the people find our own source of tremendous power and energy to be profoundly insightful and skillful in all situations. It means that we harness the power and energy of our own natural intelligence and we use that for the benefit of all. That's the only way we can ever have consummately balanced corporations, organizations and governments.

If we want our organizations to be organizations that are of benefit to all, then the people in those organizations have to have a balanced view. By the power of open intelligence, which is the root of all perceptions, we find the power that is the power to the people.

The people of the world have the power to unify the world, and that power rests in gaining ccertainty in open intelligence. When we rely on that and identify with open intelligence as the basis of our identity—rather than identifying with our ordinary thinking—then we tap into an incredible power within every human being that truly does have the power to unify the world.

Balanced View Resources

There are many resources available for anyone who is interested in knowing more about the Balanced View Training. The main sources of information are to be found at the web sites www.greatfreedom.org and www.balancedview.org. Posted there are numerous public talks, videos and books, as well as a forum where people all over the world share their experience of relying on open intelligence in daily life. All the video and audio talks offered there are free and can be easily downloaded in mp4 and mp3 format.

Also listed on the website is a schedule of Balanced View trainings offered by trainers around the world. Venues range from face-to-face training and public open meetings, to trainings and meetings offered via tele-conference bridge.

The Four Mainstays of Balanced View support everyone interested in gaining certainty in open intelligence. When confidence is inspired by the Four Mainstays—1) short moments of open intelligence, 2) the trainer, 3) the training, and 4) the worldwide community—there is increasing instinctive recognition of open intelligence until it is obvious at all times. Then there is no longer the possibility of being fooled by appearances, not during life and not upon death.

For participants who wish to contribute to Balanced View, donations are gratefully accepted; however, all are welcome, regardless of ability to contribute.

17205541R00129